A GUIDE TO
Long Island Wine Country

Wines • Vineyards • Dining • Lodging

Peter M. Gianotti

A Newsday Book

In memory of my grandfather,
Charles Giambalvo,

and my Uncle Tony,
Anthony J. Giambalvo,

and their appetite for life.

Printed by Interstate Litho
in Brentwood, N.Y.

ISBN:1885134-28-2

Table of Contents

Acknowledgments

M y thanks to Newsday publisher Raymond A. Jansen, editor Anthony Marro, managing editor Howard Schneider, marketing vice president Paul Fleishman, assistant managing editors Phyllis Singer and Mary Ann Skinner, and food editor Kari Granville for their support of this project.

I'm obliged to Alan J. Wax of Newsday for his authoritative coverage of the Long Island wine industry and contributions to this report. Credit also to photo editor Tony Jerome; design director Bob Eisner; art director Joe Toscano; copy editor Emily-Sue Sloane; and Herbie Wheeler, Sylvia Carter and Carol Bennett of the Newsday food staff.

Thanks once again to the winemakers of Long Island for their cooperation and their candor.

I'm grateful to Joseph D'Amore, Mitchell R. Berger, Margaret M. Ames, Steven M. Goldberg and Dione Lossmann, for their ongoing aid. I've shared the wine and food experiences in this book with many, and my appreciation especially goes to Betty and Jack Maggio; Ellen, Ira and Karen Travis; Catherine and Frank Rinaldi; David Fluhrer; Eileen Bruckner; Terry and Jim Bowler; and, long-distance, to Jo and Joseph Vitulli.

A toast to my mother, Lillian N. Gianotti, who, ahead of her time in all things, knew red wine was good for you long before any studies confirmed it; and to my sister, Margaret E. Gianotti, who makes all wines sparkling.

Magnums of thanks to my wife, Rita Ciolli, and to my daughters, Claire and Teresa, co-authors from the caves of Champagne to the vineyards of the East End, and all important places in between.

And a note of gratitude to my spirited assistants, Tiger and Shadow, who, threading their way through countless open bottles of wine on the kitchen and dining room tables, preferred the bouquets of cabernets.

Introduction

When Noah arrived on Mount Ararat, he planted a vineyard. In the beginning, there was wine. Some time later, corks started popping on the East End of Long Island. And in the three years since *Newsday*'s *Guide to the Wines of Long Island* was published, the local trade of turning grapes into wine has been transformed.

What for decades was viewed as a family business of boutique wineries is becoming a lure for major investors, too. Millions of dollars have poured into the region, and several well-known and respected wineries are under new ownership.

• Long Island's first winery of the modern era, the Hargrave Vineyard in Cutchogue, was sold to an Italian prince.

• Bedell Cellars, a leading producer of red wine in Cutchogue, and Corey Creek Vineyards of Southold, which built a reputation on chardonnay and merlot, both were acquired by a movie executive.

• Gristina Vineyards in Cutchogue, a key player in the first generation of wineries, was bought by a telecommunications executive.

• Laurel Lake Vineyards in Laurel has become the first Long Island winery to attract foreign capital and now is owned by a group of Chilean investors.

• Peconic Bay Winery in Cutchogue, started by a local air-traffic controller, was purchased by a New York investment manager.

And Bidwell Vineyards in Cutchogue, family-run since 1982, is for sale, in case you have about $3 million handy.

At the same time, the new Raphael winery building is rising on the south side of Main Road in Peconic at more than twice that price; the vintners of Schneider Vineyards have planted their first vines in Riverhead; and the Premium Wine Group's facility, the first to custom-make wine for vineyards without wineries, has opened in Mattituck.

This extraordinary round of activity, affecting about

one-third of Long Island's wine producers, followed the openings in the last three years of the Channing Daughters Winery in Bridgehampton, Macari Vineyards in Mattituck and Martha Clara Vineyards in Riverhead.

At the same time, production has increased, more acres are turning from yielding vegetables to nurturing grapevines, and enough ink has been spilled on the subject to float an ark.

A bottle of classic Bordeaux such as Chateau Mouton-Rothschild 1945, which is still available if you can afford it, is more than twice as old as the entire Long Island wine trade. In less time than it takes for such a wine to reach its peak, an industry started, established itself, altered the local landscape and shows the potential not only for a very long stay but to be one of the region's main tourist attractions.

The first sign announcing, "Welcome to Long Island Wine Country. Tour the Vineyards" appears just beyond Long Island Expressway exit 73, shortly after you spot the obelisk-style tower proclaiming the Tanger Outlet Centers, parts I and II. The outlets are another example of how things have changed on a stretch of land that used to be known nationally for ducklings and potatoes.

Suffolk County still is New York State's agricultural center, if you go by the value of the products the farmers produce, from nursery plants and flowers, to a score or more of edible crops. The North Fork has always been a beautiful and fertile place, where you still can see a cattle-crossing sign; the South Fork, just as productive in its own distinctive way, has the ocean beaches as further reward.

From spring through summer and deep into autumn, the twin forks attract thousands of visitors to the shore and the farmstands, to villages with antique shops and restaurants, to a big water park, an aquarium, a Christmas-tree farm, an historic homestead, a harvest festival and an old-fashioned carousel ride. The East End is a part of Long Island that seems largely removed from the rest of suburbia.

That wineries would grow in its rich soil makes sense. Today.

Reporting on the growth of Long Island's wine country has been a trip from skepticism to belief. If you were to ask 30 years ago whether it was advisable to plant grapes and make wine, you would have appeared more quixotic than inquisitive.

At the suggestion of Robert W. Greene, long-time Newsday editor, investigative reporter and four-star epicure, I first sampled a Long Island wine in the late 1970s. My recollection is that the wine needed time, and so did the vineyard.

Years ago, Bob had faith in what was then a one-winery industry. His instincts, as usual, proved right. In 1985, the Hamptons, and in 1986, the North Fork were designated as wine-growing regions by the federal government. There are 138 of these areas in the United States. Each was established based on geography, climate and the percentage of local grapes used to make the wine. Exit potatoes, enter cabernet.

The report that follows is a tour in red and white, still and sparkling, without rosé-colored glasses. Consider it a user's guide to Long Island wines, whether you choose one from the winery, a wine shop, online or from a restaurant's list.

It's also a guide to restaurants on the North and South Forks that are near the vineyards, and a directory of places to stay and to visit while you're in Long Island wine country.

There's information on each of the wineries to make your visits easier and to help you select what wines to buy. I've listed best buys and highlights. And I've reviewed hundreds of wines.

No one ever should be intimidated by a wine label or by what's in the bottle. Wine is meant to be enjoyed.

These pages are a consumer's guide to wines that are available now, some that are scheduled to be released soon, many from recent vintages and a number of older wines. Since production on Long Island, even after recent growth spurts, is comparatively limited, many of the wines are sure to vanish quickly.

Most of the wines reviewed in this book were tasted twice, at the time of their release and within the last year or so. All the wines reviewed are from the 1990s, most since 1993. Plenty of the wines, particularly from 1993, 1995 and 1997, are recommended.

The book also is meant to be used as a general reference on the subject of wine, with chapters devoted to how wine is made, techniques of wine tasting, the best ways to store wine and determining which wines pair well with different foods. I've added a glossary to help clarify the babble of "wine-speak".

Adjectives aside, early Long Island wines were notable more for their ambition than their taste. They were curiosities. The first impression from the fruit of the young vines and their rapidly released wines wasn't very good.

But, in 1988, the East End produced its first memorable vintage. And in the mid-1990s, the region experienced a series of winning years, making the North Fork and the Hamptons a destination for grape nuts as well as vacationers. As the sign outside Ternhaven Cellars in Greenport notes, "Last winery before France."

Let's go.

> Peter M. Gianotti
> Long Island, N.Y.
> February, 2001

*Louisa and Alex Hargrave in their Cutchogue vineyard,
where the modern Long Island wine industry began.*

Chapter 1

Chateau Potato

From spuds to chards

Alex Hargrave was a student of history and politics; Louisa Hargrave, of government and education. The vines of their experience were more ivy than grape.

He'd spent a summer in the Dordogne region of France while a teenager. The family with whom he stayed made their wine. Hargrave's own family, in upstate New York, was immersed in banking and law. But relatives were outside directors of the Taylor Wine Co.

She was the granddaughter of Norman Thomas, the

Socialist leader and candidate for president of the United States, a native of Cold Spring Harbor, and once summered in Spain, a nation swimming in wine.

But both were devotees of Bordeaux, Francophiles to the coeur since their student days at Harvard in the 1960s. The Hargraves wanted to make wine. And they wanted to use the grapes that yielded the best red wines in France: cabernet sauvignon, merlot, pinot noir.

"I was 23 years old when we made the decision, and 23-year-olds tend to throw themselves into projects without doing a lot of research," Louisa Hargrave recalled. "We felt we could figure it out. Because of our age, we felt it was worth a 10-year trial. We weren't concerned about failure. I'd be 33, and we could do something else."

So, in the early 1970s, they drove a Jeep Wagoneer around the country in search of their ideal vineyard. They traveled along the West Coast and through upstate New York. The couple went as far south as Virginia. Washington State and Oregon were deemed too chilly or too wet for some of the grape varieties they planned to grow. The celebrated valleys of California were too expensive. John Tompkins, a professor at Cornell University, suggested they skip planting vinifera grapes, the species of cabernet and chardonnay, in favor of sturdier hybrid varieties, which are at home upstate. But he saw that this recommendation had about as much chance as a grapevine secured in the Arctic circle. "We wouldn't grow hybrids. Everybody advised us to grow hybrids," Louisa Hargrave said. "If we weren't going to grow vinifera, we weren't going to grow grapes at all."

Tompkins then said they ought to go see a veteran farmer on Long Island who'd had some experience with grapes. The Hargraves went to Cutchogue, which certainly had the right soil for vegetables, particularly potatoes. Asparagus and cauliflower grew well there, too. Farming had been the work of the North Fork for almost 350 years. The growing season lasted more than 210 days, compared with 165 days in the Finger Lakes wine region upstate.

It was possible, if not assured, that this area, with such a climate and such good-draining soil, would be hospitable to vinifera grapes.

In 1972, on the day before Thanksgiving, the Hargraves visited the respected John Wickham at his Cutchogue

Established 1973.

farm. Wickham's family had been farming on the North Fork longer than many winemakers had been harvesting grapes in France. Among the fairly recent additions to Wickham's crops were Mediterranean varieties of grapes. "He put us in a truck and drove us to the bay, the sound, all around," said Louisa Hargrave. The conditions seemed right for growing vinifera grapes. Indeed, grapes were ripening remarkably late in the season. Alex Hargrave, who's from the Finger Lakes area, said it was as if they'd "discovered a Garden of Eden."

In this garden, the main temptations were the climate and the soil. There was plenty of sun, more than in any part of New York State. Peconic Bay, Long Island Sound and the Atlantic Ocean gave much of the East End a warm, maritime quality, keeping temperatures from turning too cold too early. The soil was well-drained, coarse, sandy loam.

But Wickham nevertheless cautioned them. "He wouldn't want a young couple to invest everything they had in an agricultural venture," Louisa Hargrave said. One of the phrases that attaches easily to winemaking is that the best way to make a small fortune is to start with a big one. The Hargraves continued their ramble through the area. "One day, we spent a whole day looking for farms, but couldn't see any crops," she added. They inquired about what was growing at every location. The real-estate agent finally said, "Don't ask. All potatoes."

But potato farms were going under. Costly spraying was necessary to curb pests, including the devastating golden nematode. Farmers began planting other crops. Or, they simply sold their land to developers for housing and minimalls.

In January 1973, the Hargraves bought a 66-acre potato farm from Edward Zuhoski on Alvah's Lane in Cutchogue. Louisa Hargrave remembered that it was $3,500 per acre, compared with $5,000 an acre on the South Fork. "For that, we got the buildings: a decrepit house, a decent barn and a potato storage building." Four months later, they planted the first 17 acres of vinifera grapes. By the following year, the Hargraves were overseeing cabernet sauvignon, pinot noir, merlot, chardonnay, riesling and sauvignon blanc.

Two years after that first planting came the Hargrave Vineyard's first vintage. The first wine was a rosé of cabernet sauvignon bottled in 1975 and released two years later. They made the rosé because it was "the solution for wine not suited for full-bodied cabernet sauvignon," said Louisa Hargrave. The oaky rosé wasn't the ideal debut. But Long Island's modern wine industry had begun. It would take 10 years to turn a profit.

Wine Country

From that old potato barn and farmhouse, the Long Island wine business has grown dramatically, and has altered the image of New York State wine. A series of high-profile purchases of Long Island wineries in the past two years has underscored the seriousness accorded the region not simply by wine lovers but by deep-pocket investors.

Many of the very early wines from the young vines were considered poor and immediately dismissed. Much trial-and-error work followed. Louisa Hargrave remembers the 1977 cabernet sauvignon as the winery's first success; the 1980 vintage produced good ones, too. The wines from other pioneers also improved. So did some of the reviews and, very slowly, the public perception of

Long Island as a wine region.

Today, 27 wine producers are in business and more are en route. More than 2,700 acres are devoted to the vineyards, which produce an estimated 500,000 cases of wine each year. Compared with the production of some of the large California wineries, that number is tiny. But volume hasn't been the goal on the East End. Moreover, as the prices of imported wines and California wines have risen, the cost of Long Island wines has become a bit more palatable to potential buyers. It has been one of the enduring ironies that consumers who eagerly insist on sampling the local wine abroad frequently have been resistant to the local product at home. A series of fine vintages in the 1990s is gradually changing that.

The growth that followed the Hargraves' effort was triggered in part by New York State's Farm Winery Act in 1976 and related bills. The laws contained tax incentives making it economically viable to run a small winery. Wineries were permitted to offer tastings and sell directly to consumers, including on Sundays.

Suffolk County boosted the industry with a farmland preservation program in which the county acquired development rights to farm properties. This way, farmers were compensated for the difference between selling the land for farm use and for other kinds of development. The first purchase was in 1977. The program signaled the ongoing transition of the agricultural economy from vegetables to grapes. The potato farms could just as easily have been a real-estate developer's delight in the vacation lands of the North Fork and the Hamptons.

In the Beginning

Before the new wave of grapevines took root on Long Island, their relatives grew in less likely places along the East Coast. The first American wines probably date to the Huguenots. The French made wine with scuppernong grapes in the South in the 1560s.

There was wine at Jamestown in 1609, and at Plymouth in 1623. The Virginia assembly tried to spur wine production by offering prizes to colonists. Vinophile Thomas Jefferson considered the New World just as vine-friendly as the Old, and encouraged grape growing. Imported cuttings

A taste of history on Route 25.

of vinifera vines were planted in Virginia in the 17th century. William Penn planted vinifera in 1683. It's generally accepted that the first grapevines on Long Island were planted in those years, too, with settlers joining with Native Americans to grow them. There is, however, no record of success in any of these ventures.

In their readings, the Hargraves found that a fellow named William Prince had a nursery in Flushing, where he tried to grow vinifera in the 1830s. But fungus ruined those grapes, which included zinfandel before it was discovered in

California. Grapes were grown on the South Fork around that time, too, though there remains no evidence of extraordinary accomplishments in winemaking. Prince also introduced the blue Isabella grape, from South Carolina, in Flushing in 1816. But that venture was ruined by mildew. Finally, he concluded that the region was too humid. Efforts by others to produce vinifera grapes, from Jamaica to Brooklyn, also failed.

"Prince turned north, to the Hudson Valley," said Alex Hargrave. "And the wine world went with him." But there are records of some wines made on Long Island in the 19th century. Whether any was worth a toast is not known. New York State eventually became the province of grapes such as concord and pink catawba. Plenty of grapes were destined for jelly, grape juice and the fruit basket instead of the wine bottle.

Early in this century, the state made recommendations about what fruits would grow best here. The source for this compilation was research conducted upstate. The idea was that if the fruits could survive the northern chill, they could endure anywhere in New York. Vinifera grapes did poorly in the upstate tests and, accordingly, weren't considered a recommended crop.

It wasn't until the 1950s that vinifera grapes were produced commercially in New York State. Winemaker Charles Fournier of Gold Seal Vineyards in the Finger Lakes region hired Konstantin Frank, an expert on the species. Fournier himself had worked with French hybrids such as aurora and seyval blanc. Frank, a viticulturalist and enologist from Ukraine, experimented. He planted rootstocks and vinifera varieties upstate. Frank succeeded with gewürztraminer and riesling.

Experiments and Growth

Around the same time, Wickham was growing table grapes on the North Fork as part of an experiment in agriculture with Cornell University. Cornell provided the plantings.

The grapes the Hargraves saw growing on Long Island were southern Mediterranean varieties. They believed that if the southern grapes could grow, so could the northern European varieties, and they, therefore, could produce premium wines. Into the earth at the Hargrave property went rootstocks that originated in Napa and Sonoma. The vineyard added cabernet franc and pinot blanc to the initial plantings.

More fields would soon be turned over to grapevines. After the Hargraves settled in, the 1980s brought Pindar Vineyards, owned by a doctor from Stony Brook; The Lenz Winery, established by restaurateurs; Mattituck Hills Winery by a local builder and The Bridgehampton Winery, founded by an advertising executive. Pindar is the largest winery on Long Island. And Lenz continues to thrive.

But The Bridgehampton Winery, which had artful labels and a carefully cultivated image, provided a harsh lesson. Most of Long Island's wine country has a fairly similar environment, and the differences among the vineyards aren't that great, compared, for example, to those in Italy or France.

The Bridgehampton Winery was situated on a South Fork site that had unsatisfactory drainage. Not that it was like sticking a vine in concrete. But it wasn't good enough. The vineyard also had areas that were uncommonly hospitable to frost in autumn and spring. Grapevines died fast. The desirable microclimate that drew winemakers to Long Island didn't envelop this piece of land. It was a mini-microclimate unto itself.

Owner Lyle Greenfield nevertheless managed to turn out some well-received wines working with The Lenz Winery. The labels were from paintings and very attractive, so much so that Bridgehampton charged visitors who wanted a label for a souvenir. It was a little thing. But you left wondering whether the economic climate had turned cold, too.

The winery failed; its last vintage was in 1992. And the stretch between Bridgehampton and Sag Harbor, no doubt fine as a wildlife refuge, still is a reminder of what can go wrong.

The Bridgehampton Winery wasn't the sole casualty. Soundview Vineyards, which had planted hybrid grapes, went under; so did the Northfork Winery, shut after tax problems. The Mattituck Hills Winery, overextended financially, closed, too. The old Mattituck Hills vineyards now are part of Macari Vineyards; Jamesport Vineyards bought the Northfork property.

The splashiest demise of a winery belongs to Le Rêve.

*Laurel Lake Vineyards was bought
by Chilean investors.*

Owner Alan Barr built a chateau-style winery on Montauk Highway in Water Mill. Although a lot of the wine wasn't made with local grapes, Barr got publicity to spare, the most prominent being a cover of Wine Spectator. The Le Rêve story ended in foreclosure, and a brief life as the bank-run Southampton Winery. Le Rêve's acreage and winery were acquired by Dr. Herodotus Damianos, owner of Pindar Vineyards. The chateau now is Duck Walk Vineyards, giving Damianos a presence north and south.

In the 1980s, the federal government recognized the Hamptons and the North Fork of Long Island as wine-producing regions. Each received the legal designation of American Viticultural Area, or AVA, from the Bureau of Alcohol, Tobacco and Firearms. The designation is similar to the "appellation" given by the French. There are 138 AVAs in the United States.

An AVA is defined by boundaries both climatic and geographic. These include soil, elevation and topography. To use the designation on a bottle of wine, 85 percent of the grapes in that wine must be from the AVA. For a wine to be labeled a varietal, such as cabernet sauvignon or chardonnay, at least 75 percent of the wine has to be from that grape.

The two AVA designations on Long Island are "North Fork of Long Island," awarded in 1986; and "The Hamptons, Long Island," in 1985. An application to designate Long Island as a whole as a new AVA currently is under consideration by the bureau. The goal is to protect the name against marketing fraud.

The two forks are distinct growing areas, courtesy of the glacier that carved out Long Island. The North Fork points northeasterly, has a moderate climate, warmer winds and, thereby, generally warmer temperatures than the South.

It also has protection afforded by the waters of Peconic Bay and Long Island Sound. The South Fork is wider and longer, and the terrain is different. The soil is heavier, denser and richer; the water table, high. The temperature can be cooler, as The Bridgehampton Winery learned. There's more fog, less sun, and the growing season can be shorter. Situating a vineyard on the South Fork requires a lot of research. Currently, three wineries operate there.

Channing Daughters Winery in Bridgehampton, Duck Walk in Water Mill and Wölffer Estate-Sagpond Vineyards in Sagaponack are the trio. Most of Long Island's wineries are on the North Fork, between Aquebogue and Greenport. The biggest concentration is in Cutchogue.

Elsewhere on Long Island, Banfi, the major Italian wine importer, has a 55-acre chardonnay vineyard in Old Brookville. It's the lone vineyard in Nassau County. For years, the wines have been made at Chateau Frank in upstate Hammondsport. But Banfi plans to use the Premium Wine Group on the North Fork to make its future wines. Loughlin Vineyards in Sayville has had its wines made by Peconic Bay Winery in Cutchogue.

The grape varieties grown on Long Island are led by chardonnay, which is by far the most planted and the most popular among wine buyers. Other white-wine grapes grown in the region include chenin blanc, gewürztraminer, pinot blanc, riesling, sauvignon blanc and viognier. The reds include cabernet franc, cabernet sauvignon, merlot, pinot noir and sangiovese.

The Next Generation

In spring 1998, Alex and Louisa Hargrave sent a second shock wave across the North Fork, one that would be followed almost immediately by others.

They were going to sell their winery and vineyard. The asking price at the time was $3.3 million.

Among the reasons given was that Alex Hargrave wanted to continue his advanced studies in Chinese linguistics after spending more than a generation in grapeworld. He was able to work only in his spare time on a linguistics project dealing with languages in existence before written records.

More than a year later, the Hargrave Vineyard was sold for about $4 million. The sale price for the Hargrave operation went up after the fairly quick sale of Peconic Bay Winery in Cutchogue.

The new owners of Hargrave Vineyard are Marco and Ann Marie Borghese. That particularly pleased the sellers. Louisa Hargrave said they were hoping for investors from a country, such as France or Italy, with long traditions of winemaking. The new owners, she said, would bring additional "credibility to the area."

The Borghese lineage is noble and can be traced to the Middle Ages. And Marco Borghese indeed is a prince, from a family that has been a patron of the arts. The Borgheses bought the property with other investors, from Florida, New York and Pennsylvania. Marco Borghese's ventures have included import-export businesses. But they've not been in the wine business. The landmark winery now is known as Castello di Borghese-Hargrave Vineyard.

At the time of the acquisition, Marco Borghese said, "I see potential here." The Borgheses are considering expanding the Hargrave repertoire of wines to include grape varieties that yield some of Italy's top wines: the nebbiolo of Barbaresco and Barolo; the sangiovese, the main grape in Chianti, and the popular dolcetto.

They're enjoying the new place. "It's beautiful country," Marco Borghese said. He's also keenly aware that the competition has intensified.

The price the Borgheses paid for the Hargrave property rose after the January 1999 acquisition of Peconic Bay Winery. Almost two decades after landing his own vineyard, Ray Blum, the former air-traffic controller at

MacArthur Airport in Islip, sold Peconic Bay. Blum's first wine appeared in 1984. The new owners of Peconic Bay are Paul and Ursula Lowerre.

Paul Lowerre, an asset manager for PaineWebber, got involved in East End vineyards two years earlier. The Lowerres purchased farmland for vineyards, spending $3 million for 147 acres in Cutchogue. They bought Peconic Bay Winery's 30 acres and winery for about $2 million. At the time, Blum held onto 40 acres of vineyard east of the Peconic property.

Six months after the sale of Peconic Bay Winery, Laurel Lake Vineyards in Laurel was sold by Michael McGoldrick, a commercial real-estate developer, who had acquired what then was the 20-acre San Andres vineyard in Laurel in 1994. The new owner of Laurel Lake is a consortium of Chilean investors. The acquisition was the first investment in the Long Island wine trade by people in the wine business abroad.

The investors, headed by industrialist Francisco Gillmore, purchased the vineyards and winery for $2.7 million, and are planning a significant expansion, tripling the production capacity.

Among the principals involved in Laurel Lake is Cesar Baeza, part-owner of the Brotherhood Winery in Washingtonville, in the Hudson Valley.

These transactions seemed like a prelude to the show-stopping double-bill that also was under way.

Michael Lynne, president and chief operating officer of New Line Cinema, purchased Corey Creek Vineyards in Southold from founders Joel and Peggy Lauber for approximately $2 million, and followed that by acquiring Bedell Cellars in Cutchogue from founders Kip and Susan Bedell for $5 million.

The Bedell deal, in January 2000, was widely viewed as signifying how ripe the North Fork is to investors, both for pursuing high-quality wines and expansion of the industry. Lynne, a wine collector and summer resident of East Hampton, and co-investors had purchased one of the region's most respected merlot producers. Winemaker Bedell agreed to stay on for five years. He and his wife established Bedell Cellars in 1980.

Lynne had looked in France and in California before moving on Corey Creek and Bedell. The Lynne purchases

North and South: Dr. Herodotus Damianos, owner of Pindar Vineyards in Peconic and Duck Walk Vineyards in Water Mill.

made headlines. But they would soon be rivaled. In August 2000, the record price paid for Bedell Cellars was broken.

Vincent Galluccio, a telecommunications executive whose career has included work with British Telecom, IBM and Metromedia Fiber Network in Europe, paid $5.2 million for Gristina Vineyards in Cutchogue.

Galluccio bought the winery and 84 acres of vineyards. He also has purchased other sites, bringing Galluccio's East End total to 211 acres. Galluccio plans to enlarge the winemaking facilities at Gristina, and is considering purchase of a fourth North Fork farm. He bought Gristina Vineyards from Connecticut physician Jerry Gristina. The Gristina family first planted the potato farm with grapes in 1983.

At the time of the sale, Galluccio, senior vice president of Metromedia Fiber Networks, Inc., in White Plains, said, "I've always wanted to do this since I was a kid." He added, "I've had this passion on hold. I've only been able to dance around this flame by visiting wineries and vineyards in every place I worked." Galluccio worked in Europe for 17 of the past 25 years.

He expects that after he has made the changes at Gristina, he'll have invested $10 million in the business. A new name is expected for what immediately was called Galluccio Estate Vineyards-Gristina Winery.

Galluccio's activity in the market isn't likely to be the end of changes in the near term. Bidwell Vineyards in Cutchogue, a Route 48 neighbor of Castello di Borghese-Hargrave Vineyard, is for sale for about $3 million. The Bidwell family has run the winery and vineyard for 17 years.

The sporting world is entering the North Fork wine industry via Leslie Alexander, the owner of the Houston Rockets in the National Basketball Association and the Houston Comets of the WNBA. Alexander has purchased three farms in Cutchogue and Mattituck. He owns 125 acres for a planned B & L Farms vineyard.

Farther west, Robert Entenmann, grandson of bakery founder William Entenmann and the former owner of the Bay Shore operation that keeps the family name, has turned his attention from thoroughbred horses to grapes.

Entenmann's Big E Farms in Riverhead, where Entenmann raised thoroughbreds after selling the bakery, has been turned into Martha Clara Vineyards. Martha Clara, named for the family matriarch, already has produced several fine wines made by Roman Roth of Wölffer Estate-Sagpond Vineyards.

Lieb Family Cellars, whose name is associated with some of the best pinot blanc produced on the East End, is putting out its own wines, made at Paumanok Vineyards, Macari Vineyards, and The Lenz Winery. In the future they will be made at Premium Wine Group in Mattituck. Mark and Kathy Lieb now sell sparkling wine, merlot, chardonnay and the crisp pinot blanc.

Dzugas Vineyards in Southold has produced a modest chardonnay, made at Bedell Cellars, and may expand.

In a dramatic entrance into the wine region, contractor John Petrocelli of Ronkonkoma, is building a $6.1 million winery, Raphael, in Peconic. Paul Pontallier, general manager of Chateau Margaux, one of the legendary producers in Bordeaux, is a consultant for the winery, which is specializing in merlot.

The list of the interested continues to grow, ⌣.
than the grapes they all hope to harvest.

The Old Field Vineyards is an ongoing work from
Christian Baiz, who expects to sell wines later this year. He
had them made at Pellegrini Vineyards and The Lenz
Winery. Old Field has produced pinot noir. Baiz expects to
have a tasting room open to the public on Main Road in
Southold, and to offer tours by appointment.

David Page and Barbara Shinn, who own the Manhattan
restaurant Home, tend Shinn Vineyards in Mattituck. They
bought 22 acres along Oregon Road in 1998 and planted
10 acres of red wine vinifera grapes last May. They plan to
turn a restored, 100-year-old barn into a winery.

Atlanta businessman Russell McCall has bought land in
Cutchogue opposite Pellegrini Vineyards and is expected to
start a vineyard there. William and Theresa Ackerman of
Manhattan, who have Internet interests, have planted 20
North Fork acres with grapes and also expect eventually to
produce wine.

Manhattan physician Charles Smithen and his wife,
Barbara, own the 50 acres of Sherwood House Vineyards.
Walter Silbernagel and family have 21 acres, and look for-
ward to producing wine.

And the country's first custom-crush winery is in the
works in Mattituck. Winemaker Russell Hearn of Pellegrini
Vineyards is among the principals in this enterprise, in
which grape growers who have no facilities to make wine
will go to the Premium Wine Group for production. About
20 percent of the area's 2,700 vineyard acres are not
owned by wineries.

In addition to Banfi, Premium has Schneider Vineyards
and Martha Clara Vineyards among its early customers.

The combined sales of Long Island's wineries now total
about $65 million per year. The bottles no longer are
curiosities. More stores sell them. They appear on more
wine lists. You can buy one on an American Airlines flight.
Or when you arrive at Disney World. When the conversation turns to the future of wine in New York State, Long
Island is the main topic.

Results of Long Island winemaking in the last decade or
so have been especially encouraging. The 1988 vintage
produced excellent wines and intensified the focus on the
region. Comparative, blind tastings of wines from

California, France and Long Island often have placed the local wines equal to or ahead of the competition.

Symposia held by Long Island winemakers have put their wines under more scrutiny. The most significant of these events involved participants from Bordeaux. The winemakers discussed similarities and differences between the two areas. The tastings that followed led to many positive reviews. A symposium on merlot brought similar results.

Since then, many Long Island wineries have collected medals in nationwide competitions. While it's easy to criticize such contests, where medals pile up faster than at the Olympics, they are an indicator.

Indeed, the tasting room at Palmer Vineyards in Aquebogue keeps a medal count on the wall, from "double-gold" to bronze. The winery's total is in the hundreds. Palmer wines are marketed locally, as well as in Asia and Europe.

At a wine tasting around the time that the Hargrave Vineyard went on the market, the veteran of 27 growing seasons, Alex Hargrave, observed that in the past 10 years, "we've had five outstanding vintages and some very good ones." To have that many "is a measure of the power of the Long Island growing region." One that began with a $3.99 rosé.

But just as the wine industry inspired by the Hargraves has changed, so have the Hargraves' lives. They have divorced. Alex Hargrave lives in Connecticut. Louisa Hargrave is a wine consultant on the North Fork.

She specializes in starting vineyards.

Chapter 2

A Harvest
of Wineries

Visiting the vineyards

The wineries of Long Island are as different from
one another as the wines they produce. They vary
dramatically in size, approach and style of wines.
At one winery, you'll find a repertoire ranging from dry to
sweet to sparkling, and from red to white to blush. At
another, you may find a single varietal produced.

Most of the wineries are open to the public, and many
offer tours, whether self-guided, guided or by appointment
only. Such a tour is a worthwhile way to be introduced to
this expanding wine region.

But be realistic about how many wineries you plan to
visit on a given day. You could see all three South Fork

wineries in one day. But visiting the North Fork requires some planning, just to manage your time.

Decide what kind of tour, if any, you prefer, and pick the wineries accordingly. Typically, group tours last less than an hour before you wind up in the tasting room. Self-guided tours, invariably quick, also can be quite good.

Be just as judicious in the tasting room. Most wines may be sampled free. There usually is a modest charge for a rare or more expensive wine. In most cases, you'll have a chance to try whites and reds, from the regular bottlings and sometimes from the reserves, and perhaps a rosé or a dessert wine.

As you would at the dinner table, start with white and move on to red, from young wine to older wine, from dry to sweet. There may be crackers to nibble on and help clear your palate between wines.

If you intend to sample a lot of wines at several wineries, be sure your encounters are swirl-sniff-sample-and-spit affairs. Tasting isn't the same as draining the glass. It's wise to do your drinking at home. The wineries offer for sale all the wines they pour.

The tasting rooms are accessible by wheelchair. But not all of them are situated next to the parking facilities. You may have to travel a short distance.

What follows is an overview of the vineyards and wineries, with some details about each one.

Banfi Old Brookville Vineyards
1111 Cedar Swamp Rd., Old Brookville
516-626-9200; 516-626-6282 (fax)

An Elizabethan-style mansion is the headquarters of Banfi Vintners, the major wine importer and producer of the respected Castello Banfi wines in Italy. These include the stirring red blend Summus and the justly respected Brunello di Montalcino. The Old Brookville place, nestled among some of Long Island's pricier communities on the Gold Coast, is very much an estate.

The property is about 127 acres. It had been crop-growing land for Young's Farm Stand. Banfi grows only chardonnay grapes. The first plantings date to 1982. The vineyard is 55 acres, or at least one acre for each room in the manor house, whose earlier owners included Margaret

Emerson, daughter of the inventor of Bromo Seltzer, and
Frederick Lundy, the restaurateur whose Sheepshead Bay
namesake is a local landmark.

The 2000 vintage of Banfi Old Brookville chardonnay
is expected to be vinified at the Premium Wine Group in
Mattituck. Previously, the grapes were crushed at Duck
Walk Vineyards in Water Mill and then transported to
Chateau Frank in Hammondsport, N.Y., in the Finger
Lakes wine-producing region, where the wine was made.

Poor weather did away with what would have been
Banfi's 1999 vintage. The most current available vintage
is the 1998.

Banfi Old Brookville used to make a blanc de blancs
méthode Champenoise sparkling wine, complete with three
years of bottle aging, but that has been discontinued.

The Old Brookville operation is the sole commercial
vineyard in Nassau County. It is closed to the public.

Bedell Cellars

Main Road (Route 25), Cutchogue
631-734-7537; 631-734-5788 (fax)
www.bedellcellars.com

Bedell Cellars started in 1980 in potato territory. But
Kip Bedell, who ran a fuel-oil company in Nassau
County, was making wine in his West Hempstead base-
ment in the 1970s.

In Cutchogue, Kip and Susan Bedell began by planting

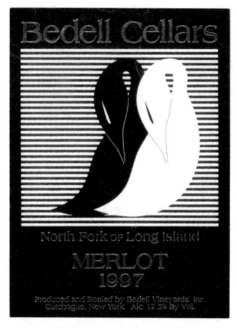

seven acres. Bedell's first North Fork vintage was in 1985, when Hurricane Gloria whipped across Long Island. The soft-spoken Bedell recalls speeding up that harvest.

Over the years, Bedell has established himself as one of Long Island's premier merlot producers. His reserve merlots are age-worthy wines. Bedell excels in cabernet sauvignon and reserve chardonnays, too.

Merlot is planted in about one-third of the 30-acre vineyard, and the winery sells more of it than any other varietal or blend. Bedell also grows cabernet sauvignon, chardonnay and smaller plots of cabernet franc, gewürztraminer, riesling and viognier.

His red blend, Cupola, is the newest creation, made primarily with cabernet sauvignon, plus cabernet franc and merlot. There have been three vintages of Cupola, the latest being the stellar 1997. Three cupolas highlight the design of the century-old building, too.

Simpler and satisfactory blends from Bedell include Main Road Red, Main Road White and Cygnet, which are sold at bargain prices. The pickup truck on the label of the Main Road wines may be on the premises when you visit. Bedell also produces a ripe dessert wine named EIS, and a raspberry wine, which is the basis of a cookbook sold at the winery.

Bedell Cellars, housed in what once was a potato barn, is undergoing an extensive overhaul following its acquisition from Kip and Susan Bedell in 2000 by Michael Lynne, president and chief operating officer of New Line Cinema. Lynne also purchased Corey Creek Vineyards in Southold.

Bedell is expected to remain winemaker for at least the next four years, in effect freed from running the business end of the winery. Bedell Cellars produces about 8,500 cases per year.

The tasting room is open daily, from 11 a.m. to 5 p.m., except Christmas, Thanksgiving and Easter. Tours are limited to 10 or more and should be scheduled two days in advance.

Bidwell Vineyards

Route 48, Cutchogue
631-734-5200

Bidwell Vineyards was established in 1982, and it always has been very much a family operation.

Currently, the Bidwell brothers, Bob, Kerry and Jim, run the winery, which was started by their parents. Bidwell Vineyards, however, may be the next winery to be

Estate Bottled
1997

BIDWELL

BARREL FERMENTED CHARDONNAY

NORTH FORK OF LONG ISLAND

ALCOHOL 12.5% BY VOLUME

sold. The brothers have other interests to pursue after a career in wine. Bidwell Vineyards has been on the market, with a price tag of $2.99 million. Bidwell's first vintage was in 1986. The 37-acre vineyard is divided among chardonnay, sauvignon blanc, merlot, cabernet sauvignon and white riesling. The winery has excelled in crisp white wines, particularly an uncommonly fruity sauvignon blanc, which has been made here since 1990.

The newest wine is called Claret, a term the British use for Bordeaux, that blends cabernet sauvignon, merlot and cabernet franc.

Over the years, Bidwell wines have been released in two stages. The first, with a spare label and black type, is an unblended and unfiltered preview, for sale at the winery. The second release, still unfiltered but occasionally blended, receives the regular label. The wines emphasize the qualities of the fruit and suggest a minimalist approach to vinification.

Bidwell's wines are sold primarily at the winery, but they are available at some shops on Long Island.

The tasting room is open daily, from 11 a.m. to 6 p.m. It's an airy, sunny space. Among the decorations is a poster advertising Armagnac. The tasting room opened in 1996. It was "built by growing grapes," Bob Bidwell said. Tours are by appointment.

Castello di Borghese-Hargrave Vineyard

Route 48, Cutchogue
631-734-5111
www.castellodiborghese.com

The modern Long Island wine industry started here. Alex and Louisa Hargrave planted their first vineyard in 1973, and their name became synonymous with local wine. In 1999, the Hargraves sold the winery and the property to Marco and Ann Marie Borghese of Philadelphia.

Marco Borghese has been involved in the import-export business there and in New York City, and by training is an engineer. Although he doesn't use the title, Borghese is a prince, with a noble lineage that dates back centuries in Italy. Some of his relatives are in the wine trade in Italy.

The Hargraves' imprint is on wines through the 1999

vintage, and they've provided assistance in the 2000 harvest. At the time of the sale, the Hargraves agreed to be consultants to the vineyard for two years.

The winemaker at Castello di Borghese-Hargrave Vineyard is Mark Terry, who worked with the Hargraves for 15 years.

Wines from this vineyard that are reviewed in this book are listed as Hargrave wines. Those are the labels by which you'll find them. The new label, highlighting the Castello di Borghese name above that of Hargrave Vineyard, starts with the 1998 pinot noir.

The Borgheses expect to remodel the building that houses the tasting room. When the Hargraves left, so did the Tiffany stained-glass window with the image of Millet's "The Sower." But the Borgheses already have added an art gallery on the premises.

And production capacity has increased. The Hargrave output of 11,000 cases could be tripled. Borghese expects to plant five acres of sangiovese grapes, and one acre each of nebbiolo and dolcetto. Sangiovese is the grape of Chianti, nebbiolo of Barbaresco, Barolo and Gattinara. Dolcetto is a favorite of southwest Piedmont.

While sangiovese is grown elsewhere on the North Fork,

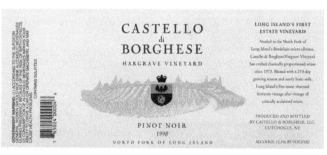

nebbiolo has been tried only at the Cornell Horticultural Research Center in Riverhead. About 20 of the Hargrave Vineyard's 84 acres are planted with grapevines.

But the introduction of these stellar Italian grapes isn't expected to alter dramatically the French character of so much of the Castello di Borghese-Hargrave portfolio. The winery's current highlights include barrel-fermented chardonnays, merlots and pinot noir.

Some of the Hargrave Vineyard's acreage is leased to a local farmer who grows vegetables.

The tasting room is open 10 a.m. to 6 p.m. Monday to Saturday; from 11 a.m. to 6 p.m. Sunday. Tours are by appointment.

Channing Daughters Winery

1927 Scuttlehole Rd., Bridgehampton
631-537-7224
www.channingdaughters.com

C hanning Daughters opened in 1997. This is the newest winery on the South Fork. It's a 25-acre vineyard that winemaker Larry Perrine figures will grow to 40. Perrine, one of Long Island's senior winemakers, plans to specialize in fresh, lighter wines similar to those made in northern Italy.

The vineyard includes pinot grigio, Tocai Friuliano, pinot blanc and the early-ripening red varietal grape, dolcetto. The winery's first releases were a chardonnay made at Peconic Bay Winery from grapes selected by Perrine, and a merlot made at The Lenz Winery.

Since then, Channing Daughters has produced red and white wines from vineyard sites named Scuttlehole, Brick Kiln and Sculpture Garden.

Walter Channing's large wooden sculptures, made from tree trunks and roots, rise from the vineyard. Channing has a passion for working with discarded materials, whether wood from the demolished Hudson Piers or from roots and tree trunks slated to be plowed on the East End. Some of Channing's art is reproduced on the labels of the winery, which is named for his four children.

Channing is a venture capitalist whose firm concentrates on managed care, health care and biotechnology. In his other life as an artist, he has a studio in Manhattan. His works have been exhibited in the United States and in Europe. The winery has produced merlot and chardonnay, and a blend called Fresh Red.

Perrine is managing partner at Channing Daughters. His Channing Perrine label appears on sauvignon blanc and riesling from grapes at the Mudd, Rolling Ridge and Oregon Road vineyards on the North Fork.

Among the attractions at this winery is its location. The vineyards are situated amid the cornfields on the road between Bridgehampton and Sag Harbor. The tasting room is open daily, from 11 a.m. to 5 p.m.

Corey Creek Vineyards

Main Road (Route 25), Southold
631-765-4168; 631-765-1845 (fax)
www.coreycreek.com

Corey Creek Vineyards was among the wineries that changed hands in the last couple of years. It was bought in 1999 by film executive Michael Lynne, who subsequently purchased Bedell Cellars, too.

Corey Creek, situated between the tidal inlets of the

1 9 9 8

COREY CREEK
VINEYARDS

CHARDONNAY
North Fork of Long Island

PRODUCED & BOTTLED BY PALMER VINEYARDS, AQUEBOGUE, NEW YORK, EXCLUSIVELY FOR COREY CREEK VINEYARDS   750 ML WHITE WINE   ALC. 12% BY VOL.

GOVERNMENT WARNING: (1). ACCORDING TO THE SURGEON GENERAL, WOMEN SHOULD NOT DRINK ALCOHOLIC BEVERAGES DURING PREGNANCY BECAUSE OF THE RISK OF BIRTH DEFECTS. (2). CONSUMPTION OF ALCOHOLIC BEVERAGES IMPAIRS YOUR ABILITY TO DRIVE A CAR OR OPERATE MACHINERY, AND MAY CAUSE HEALTH PROBLEMS.   CONTAINS SULFITES

Corey and Richmond creeks, was founded in 1981 by Joel and Peggy Lauber. Earlier, Joel Lauber ran an advertising agency. After he sold the agency, he consulted for a while.

The Laubers had a residence on the North Fork. The idea of owning a vineyard-winery had three-way appeal for them: The wine business was substantial; the local government was favorably disposed to it; and it was a good alternative to making a living in marketing in the area.

So, the Laubers bought land and sold wine grapes. They planted 14 acres of chardonnay and two acres of pinot noir and gewürztraminer in 1981. Three years later, they added five acres of merlot and two of cabernet franc. Corey Creek now totals 30 acres.

The Laubers found the grapes were so good that they decided to go into wine production themselves. Corey Creek's early wines, from the 1993 vintage, were immediate successes. Corey Creek chardonnays were made at Palmer Vineyards, the merlots at Pellegrini Vineyards.

The current winemaker is Eric Fry of The Lenz Winery. Corey Creek's yearly production is 4,000 cases.

Corey Creek's tasting room offers a fine view of the vineyard. The room opens onto a deck that is a pleasant spot for lingering. The tasting room is open from 11 a.m. to 5 p.m. Sunday to Friday, and 11:30 a.m. to 6 p.m. on Saturday. There are no tours.

Duck Walk Vineyards

Montauk Highway (Route 27), Water Mill
631-726-7555
www.duckwalk.com

Duck Walk Vineyards is the South Fork sibling of Pindar Vineyards. They're both owned by Dr. Herodotus Damianos.

The Stony Brook physician established Duck Walk in 1994. He acquired what had been the Le Rêve winery, which had folded and then briefly operated as the Southampton Winery, run by Barclay's Bank.

You can't miss the place, which seems to erupt on Montauk Highway. The owner of Le Rêve had the building designed to emulate a Norman chateau. Even if it doesn't immediately transport you to France, the building is a distinctive sight as you turn from Southampton into Water Mill.

Duck Walk has acreage on the North Fork as well as flanking the winery. The South Fork plantings include pinot gris, pinot meunier and muscat. Damianos replanted the neglected vineyards on the Duck Walk site.

Damianos' son Jason is the winemaker at Duck Walk, succeeding Mark Friszolowski, who, while Pindar winemaker, also made the Duck Walk wines. Jason Damianos is expanding the line. Duck Walk's repertoire includes several well-priced, light and medium-bodied blends, both red and white, chardonnay, merlot, cabernet sauvignon, pinot noir, pinot gris and that rarity, pinot meunier.

In addition, Damianos makes a dessert wine, called Aphrodite, with gewürztraminer. And Duck Walk has a blueberry-based version of Port, made with wild Maine blueberries.

The tasting room is open seven days, from 11 a.m. to 6 p.m. Informative tours of the winery are scheduled at noon, 2 p.m. and 4 p.m., with more tours added during the summer season.

Galluccio Estate Vineyards-Gristina Winery

24385 Main Rd. (Route 25), Cutchogue
631-734-7089; 631-734-7114 (fax)
www.gristinawines.com

The changes are coming rapidly at one of Long Island's early wineries. Galluccio-Gristina is an unfolding story.

Gristina Vineyards was purchased last year by

Vincent Galluccio, who has ambitious plans to expand the winery's production, plantings and repertoire, as well as raising its profile. The name of the new operation may change, too. And there's a new winemaker, Charles Girard.

Gristina was started in 1983 by physician and wine collector Jerry Gristina. He favored Bordeaux and Burgundy, and planned to produce cabernet sauvignon, merlot, pinot noir and chardonnay. The first grapevines were planted in 1984. Over the years, Gristina made some very big wines. The top ones have carried the "Andy's Field" designation, which refers to a gravelly and sandy bloc where the vineyard's finest grapes grow and to Gristina family member Andy Criscoulo. The grapes

that grow there have been hand-picked.

Originally, the vineyard sold its fruit. Gristina released its own first vintage in 1988, and the winery's cabernet sauvignon from that year remains a benchmark, still drinking very well. The 1988 chardonnay also was well-received. Wines from the 1993, 1995 and 1997 vintages are made to last years. Adam Suprenant made the wines in recent years. He and Galluccio parted ways in January.

Among the new arrivals in the vineyard after the purchase by Galluccio are malbec, petit verdot and viognier. The winery has produced approximately 26,000 cases from the year 2000 vintage. That compares with Gristina's 5,000 cases. Galluccio has received a great deal of attention with full-page color ads in Wine

Spectator, promotion on a scale no Long Island winery had ever done. The tasting room is open from 11 a.m. to 6 p.m. daily. Tours are by appointment.

Jamesport Vineyards

Main Road (Route 25), Jamesport
631-722-5256

The wines of Jamesport Vineyards make up an extensive and diversified portfolio. And the winery is doing well in this, its second life.

The winery was rescued in 1986 by Ron Goerler Sr., a Syosset businessman whose family operates a brass and plumbing supply company.

Goerler acquired the vineyard of the liquidated Northfork Winery. Earlier, the land hosted a fruit farm. Goerler already owned acreage in Cutchogue, which produces the grapes from which the winery's Cox Lane chardonnays are made. The new Jamesport winery was born of the two locations.

Goerler and his son, Ron Jr., sold fruit from the Early Rising Farm, their 60-acre property in Cutchogue. The vineyards at Jamesport date to 1981, making them among the North Fork's oldest.

Jamesport Vineyards makes chardonnay, riesling, cabernet sauvignon, cabernet franc, pinot noir, a sparkling wine, dessert wines, fortified wine; red, white and rosé blends, and a distinctive sauvignon blanc, which is becoming the winery's big grape.

Winemaker Sean Capiaux is leading Jamesport into a niche of softer, balanced wines, led by the sauvignon blanc, chardonnay and cabernet franc. He also fashioned a very rich, sweet and impressive late-harvest riesling

from the 1998 vintage. The white Port made with pinot
blanc is another singular selection. Jamesport's production is about 5,000 cases.

Visitors arrive at a converted barn that has been
standing for 150-plus years. The tasting room is open
seven days, from 10 a.m. to 5:30 p.m. Tours are informal
and available upon request.

Laurel Lake Vineyards

3165 Main Rd. (Route 25), Laurel
631-298-1420; 631-298-1405 (fax)
www.laurellakewines.com

Laurel Lake Vineyards has entered a new era following
its sale in 1999 to a group of Chilean investors and
wine producers.

The quality of the wines at this bright and striking winery was uneven during the mid-to-late 1990s. But Laurel
Lake released a big reserve cabernet sauvignon earlier this

year and made flavorful barrel-
fermented chardonnay. Under
the new owners, the winery
expects to produce a red blend
that could become its signature
bottle. The winemaker is Rolf
Achterberg. Among the buyers
is Cesar Baeza, co-owner of the
Brotherhood Winery upstate.

Laurel Lake is situated close
to wetlands, and its vineyard is
alive with chardonnay. This had
been the San Andres vineyard,
which commercial real-estate
developer Michael McGoldrick
purchased in 1994. The winery
was built in 1997. Laurel Lake
totals 23 acres, of which 13
are planted with chardonnay.
But the new owners have
bought a 40-acre farm nearby
and anticipate tripling the winery's production capacity. In
addition, Laurel Lake started a

nursery where sangiovese vines have been planted.

The tasting room has a stylish, vintage bar. The deck makes for a leisurely visit on a sunny afternoon, overlooking the vineyard. The winery is open daily, from 11 a.m. to 6 p.m. Tours are by appointment.

The Lenz Winery

Main Road (Route 25), Peconic
631-734-6010
www.lenzwine.com

A vintage ad for The Lenz Winery took as its inspiration the famous perspective on New York City that appeared on a cover of The New Yorker magazine. The foreground is Lenz, then it moves briskly to the rest of Long Island, Manhattan, New Jersey, Napa, the Pacific and Asia.

The Lenz Winery, a group of countrified buildings around a courtyard, does have a world view, and its wines have competed well in blind tastings with the best imports, red or white.

Lenz has been at the forefront of Long Island winemaking almost since the beginning. The Lenz Winery was among Long Island's first four, established in 1978 by Peter and Patricia Lenz, restaurateurs known for their well-received place, A Moveable Feast.

They started with gewürztraminer and pinot noir, and went on to chardonnay, cabernet sauvignon and merlot, and they produced blends, too. These varietals still are the core of the winery.

By 1988, the couple decided on other pursuits, and leased their namesake winery to management consultant

Peter Carroll, who subsequently bought the property. The changes that followed were significant, notably the addition of winemaker Eric Fry.

Carroll, Fry, vineyard manager Sam McCullough and marketing director Tom Morgan, a veteran of Lenz from the start, transformed the operation by their scientific viticultural approach, invigorating and restoring the property. They've created wines with a pronounced French style. The finesse extends from the chardonnay and merlot to excellent sparkling wines.

Fry talks about the wines with Burgundian zest, extolling earthy flavors and "funky" aromas. Among the finest of the Lenz wines is the 1997 Estate Selection Merlot. And Fry still makes a zesty, Alsatian-style gewürztraminer.

The Lenz Winery is open Monday to Friday, 10 a.m. to 5 p.m.; 6 p.m. on weekends. Informal tours are available. More detailed tours are by appointment.

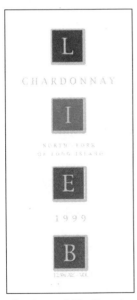

Lieb Family Cellars

35 Cox Neck Rd., Mattituck
631-734-1100
www.liebcellars.com

The Lieb name is familiar to devotees of crisp and refreshing pinot blanc. During the 1990s, Lieb vineyards' grapes contributed to the region's top pinots.

Now comes Lieb Family Cellars, with pinot blanc, chardonnay, merlot and sparkling wine released under the family label. The Lieb vineyards total about 50 acres, with the pinot blanc plantings of Alsatian vines dating to 1983. Currently, the Lieb grapes include chardonnay, merlot, cabernet sauvignon and cabernet franc, plus a little malbec and petit verdot.

Lieb Family Cellars and Lieb Vineyard are owned by Mark and Kathy Lieb. They bought their first 20-acre vineyard in 1992.

Mark Lieb is co-owner of the Premium Wine Group, the custom-crush facility in Mattituck. Early Lieb wines were made at Paumanok Vineyards, Macari Vineyards and The Lenz Winery. The next generation of Lieb wines will be made at Premium, which is situated near the vineyard.

The Lieb Family Cellars tasting room also is at the Mattituck operation, which is off Route 48. It is expected to be open to the public in spring 2001.

1999
Loughlin Vineyards
South Main Street & Meadowcroft
Sayville, NY 11782

Chardonnay
New York

DRY WHITE TABLE WINE
PRODUCED AND BOTTLED BY PECONIC BAY VINEYARDS INC.
CUTCHOGUE, LONG ISLAND, NEW YORK

ALCOHOL 12% BY VOLUME

Loughlin Vineyards

South Main Street, Sayville
631-589-0027

When Bernard Loughlin came out of the U.S. Army in 1946, he bought 15 acres in Sayville. The family planted 800 graftings on some of the acreage on Memorial Day, 1983.

What began as a hobby now is the source of about 800 cases of wine. The wines are made at Peconic Bay Winery in Cutchogue.

"People on the North Fork couldn't believe we could grow grapes on the south side," said Loughlin. "We put in plants and kept adding." For a time, he sold the grapes to the since-departed Le Rêve winery in Water Mill and then to Peconic Bay.

The vineyard is about five acres. It's planted with chardonnay, riesling and a small amount of cabernet sauvignon. Loughlin produces a blush wine called South Bay Breeze.

You reach Loughlin via a winding road after entering the Meadowcroft estate. The vineyard abuts the former estate of John Ellis Roosevelt, cousin of Theodore Roosevelt.

Loughlin wines are sold primarily in and around Sayville. The vineyard is open on weekends from May 1 to Election Day for informal tours, tastings and sales, from 11 a.m. to 5 p.m.

Macari Vineyards

150 Bergen Ave., Mattituck
631-298-0100; 631-298-8373 (fax)
www.macariwines.com

Joseph Macari Sr. is in the real-estate business, based in Jackson Heights, N.Y., and he used to make wine and sell it in Corona. But he has owned farmland on the North Fork for decades. The Macari property now totals 370 acres, making him one of the local industry's biggest landholders.

A major winery, artfully mixing the post-modern and the traditional, is Macari Vineyards' centerpiece. The winery building opened in 1998. Macari Vineyards was established where the Mattituck Hills Winery used to be.

The winery may have been a while in the making, but it had an immediately impressive debut. Macari Vineyards quickly and successfully established itself as a consistent producer of wines, red and white, as well as successful dessert and sparkling wines. The winemaker at Macari is José Montilla.

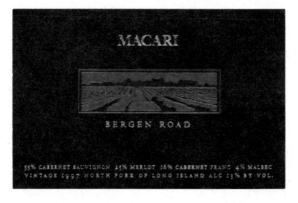

Joseph Jr., heads the winery with his wife Alexandra. The emphasis has been on particularly careful tending of the soil and the vines, using environmentally friendly techniques.

The releases are topped by a ripe red blend called Bergen Road, an ice wine called Essencia and barrel-fermented chardonnays. The more modest Collina 48 is a satisfying red table wine.

The tasting room is open 11 a.m. to 5 p.m. daily. Tours are by appointment.

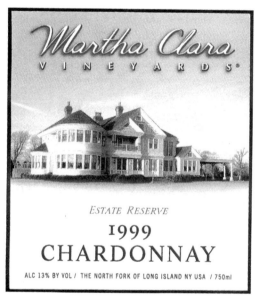

Martha Clara Vineyards

6155 Sound Ave., Riverhead
631-298-0075
www.marthaclaravineyards.com

The Entenmann name, long associated with chocolate-covered doughnuts and crumb cake visible through the clear window of the bakery box, now is part of Long Island wine lore.

Martha Clara Vineyards is named for the mother of owner Robert Entenmann. The Entenmann family sold the Bay Shore baking company in 1978. In 1995, Robert Entenmann started planting vinifera grapes on his thoroughbred horse farm in Riverhead. Earlier, the land had been a potato farm.

The new vineyard already is a big player. Wines carrying the Martha Clara label so far include reserve chardonnay, chardonnay, viognier, riesling, semillon and gewürztraminer, all successes. They've been made by Roman Roth of Wölffer Estate-Sagpond Vineyards in Sagaponack.

The Martha Clara winery is under construction in Riverhead. By summer 2001, a tasting room is expected to be open at the Sound Avenue address, in a renovated barn. Work should be completed on the winery on the Big E Farm property by 2002.

Meanwhile, Martha Clara wines are available at stores and online. The mailing address for Martha Clara currently is P.O. Box 124, Mattituck, N.Y. 11952.

Osprey's Dominion Winery

Main Road (Route 25), Peconic
631-765-6188; 631-765-1903 (fax)
www.ospreysdominion.com

The osprey's dominion is the sky. And on a sunny weekend afternoon, you may see Bill Tyree flying overhead in a classic biplane. He and Bill Koehler, both pilots, are the co-owners of Osprey's Dominion Winery.

On land, Osprey's Dominion is 90 acres. The operation started in 1986, selling grapes. Wine production began in 1993. The winery has an eclectic portfolio, one that has become a bit more refined recently.

Your choices range from varieties of chardonnay to merlot and cabernet sauvignon, to a Port. There are several popular, fun wines made with strawberries, peaches and cherries; and a spice wine, which may be the lone Long Island wine that is improved by a visit to the microwave.

Winemaker Peter Silverberg's boldest signature is on a vigorous, appealing red blend appropriately called Flight.

At the lighter end of the wine spectrum, he produces a fresh and fruity gamay nouveau.

The tasting room is a busy place. It's open daily, from 11 a.m. to 6 p.m. Tours are available on request. There's outdoor seating, so you can enjoy the view of the vineyards. Or perhaps an impromptu air show.

Palmer Vineyards

108 Sound Ave., Aquebogue
631-722-9463; 631-722-5364 (fax)
www.palmervineyards.com

Palmer Vineyards is Long Island's international winery, with bottles available in Westin Hotels, Disney World and Las Vegas. They're sold in Canada, Scandinavia, Switzerland and the United Kingdom.

And, if you're in China, you may recognize the name there, too. Robert Palmer is an advertising executive, and he has marketed well, giving Palmer one of the higher profiles among East End wineries. The winery started in 1986. The vineyards are 125 acres.

Winemaker Tom Drozd and his immediate predecessor, Dan Kleck, have made remarkably consistent wines for the label, especially chardonnays. Their styles have varied, but the chardonnays are very reliable.

The house's two chardonnays, one that's full-bodied and barrel-fermented and another that's tank-fermented and crisp, will give you a good idea of contrasting styles under one roof.

Drozd also makes highly recommended special reserve bottlings of red and white blends, and his late-harvest gewürztraminer has been a luscious success.

Palmer offers an informative self-guided tour of the winemaking areas, allowing you to move along at your own pace en route to the tasting room. That destination is appointed to resemble an English pub, but it's wine that flows as if from a font. The tasting room is open daily, from 11 a.m. to 5 p.m.

Paumanok Vineyards

Main Road (Route 25), Aquebogue
631-722-8800; 631-722-5110 (fax)
www.paumanokvineyards.com

Charles Massoud grew up in Lebanon and studied economics in France and at the Wharton School. His family was in the hotel and restaurant business. Ursula Massoud's family still has vineyards of riesling and sylvaner in Germany.

Charles was a marketing specialist at IBM for 22 years. Working in Kuwait, where alcohol isn't welcome, Massoud of necessity made his own wine. The first, in 1972, was a rosé enjoyed by the expatriate community. Of course, it was dry.

The Massouds have been at work in Aquebogue on what had been a potato farm since 1983. Their home is across from the winery and the tasting room.

In many ways, theirs is a European-style operation, from the way the vines are planted to the flavors of the wines themselves. Paumanok is 52 acres. The winery production is limited to fewer than 8,000 cases per year.

In the mid-to-late '90s, Massoud made a series of memorable wines, particularly big reds and elegant dessert wines. Look especially for the 1995 Tuthills Lane Limited Edition Cabernet Sauvignon and the 1998 Late Harvest Sauvignon Blanc.

The winery itself is housed in a vintage potato barn that has been renovated. From the tasting room, situated atop the barrel cellar, you look onto the vineyards, where cabernet sauvignon, merlot, cabernet franc, chardonnay, Johannisberg riesling, sauvignon blanc and the region's sole vines of chenin blanc are planted.

Informal tours are available upon request on weekends, from Memorial Day to Labor Day. Call in advance to arrange for a weekday tour.

Peconic Bay Winery

Main Road (Route 25), Cutchogue
631-734-7361; 631-734-5867 (fax)
www.peconicbaywinery.com

The sale of Peconic Bay Winery in early 1999 kicked off a remarkable buying spree on Long Island.

Peconic Bay, established in 1980 by Ray Blum, was sold to Paul and Ursula Lowerre. Changes at the winery have continued ever since, notably the arrival of veterans of the Long Island wine industry such as general manager Matthew Gillies and winemaker Greg Gove. The 1999 vintage will be the first one totally under the new management team.

Blum, who was an air-traffic controller at MacArthur Airport, initially sold Peconic Bay grapes. He continues to grow grapes on his own nearby site. The first Peconic Bay vintage was made at The Lenz Winery in 1984. Winemaking commenced on the premises five years later. Peconic Bay produced about 5,000 cases annually.

Peconic Bay's whites generally were more successful than its reds. But during Blum's winemaking, the best wine was a 1995 merlot named Epic Acre from a bloc you could see from the tasting room. Some Sandy Hill

chardonnay also merited praise.

The winery is on the south side of Route 25, along one of the busier stretches of the road. A shopping center is across the street, so at first the winery's venue doesn't seem very countrified. But it has a pretty view of the vineyards. Peconic Bay's tasting room is open 11 a.m. to 5 p.m. daily. Tours are by appointment.

Pellegrini Vineyards

Route 25, Cutchogue
631-734-4111; 631-734-4159 (fax)
www.pellegrinivineyards.com

Bob Pellegrini is a corporate designer, and his winery has a distinctive image. It's a striking, three-building arrangement around a courtyard. The place evokes a modern view of the North Fork. You'll never mistake it for a potato barn.

Pellegrini first got involved in the wine trade on the North Fork in 1983, and was associated with what became Gristina Vineyards. After a split with Gristina, Pellegrini purchased what had been Island Vineyards. The first Pellegrini vintage was in 1992.

The vineyard grows cabernet sauvignon, merlot, cabernet franc, chardonnay and gewürztraminer.

Production winemaker Charles Flatt and consulting winemaker Russell Hearn specialize in Bordeaux-style reds and full-bodied chardonnays. Pellegrini's Vintner's Pride label denotes the winery's top varietals and blends. The red blend dubbed Encore and the dessert wine Finale are highlights in the portfolio. The East End Select series of reds and whites is the house's less ambitious, less expensive wine.

The handsome winery's architecture offers a contrast between the contemporary and the traditional. It's a pretty site, too, whether your perspective is from the gazebo in the vineyard or from the winery itself.

Pellegrini recently bought about 50 acres of vineyard land, adding to the 30 around the winery. The South Harbor site, approximately 16 acres, is being planted with red wine grapes. The Richmond Creek vineyard, more than 30 acres, is set for red as well as for gewürztraminer, the grape that yields Finale.

The Pellegrini tasting room is open daily, from 11 a.m. to 5 p.m. Tours are self-guided. Guided tours for groups should be scheduled in advance.

PELLEGRINI
VINEYARDS

VINTNER'S PRIDE

F I N A L E

WHITE TABLE WINE

NORTH FORK OF
LONG ISLAND

1 9 9 8

Alcohol 11% by Volume

Pindar Vineyards

Main Road (Route 25), Peconic
631-734-6200; 631-734-6205 (fax)
www.pindar.net

Pindar Vineyards is one of Long Island's earliest wineries and has grown to be the biggest: 80,000 cases and more than 400 acres.

Pindar is owned by Dr. Herodotus Damianos, who also owns Duck Walk Vineyards in Water Mill. The doctor's prescription for success, from production to marketing, is different from that of most other Long Island wineries. Pindar, which takes its name from the Greek poet, is no boutique.

Actually, it could be a couple of wineries under a single name. The repertoire of winemaker Mark Friszolowski is the most diverse in the region. At last count, 17 varieties of grapes were planted.

The winery, in effect, has taken a split-level approach. Wines such as Winter White, Autumn Gold, Spring Splendor, Summer Blush and Sweet Scarlett are uncomplicated and inexpensive, frequently criticized and more often purchased.

Then, there are the dependable varietals, especially merlot and chardonnay, in regular and reserve bottlings, with an oaky, California-style chardonnay in the mix, too.

The summit at Pindar is the Bordeaux-style blend Mythology, which can be exceptional, ranking high on the all-Long Island list. Friszolowski also fashions a lush, deluxe ice wine from Johannisberg riesling, and he has produced a stirring syrah. In a lighter realm is the gamay Beaujolais, as well as the diverting pinot meunier.

By the sheer volume of what it produces, Pindar's

impact on the local industry is potent: "Dr. Dan," as Damianos is called, has gotten a lot of people to sample Long Island wines, and an extraordinary range of them, too. There is something for pretty much every taste, each poured here with enthusiasm.

The first Pindar wines were planted in 1979. The initial wines were made in 1983. Enologist Dimitri Tchelistcheff, son of the legendary Beaulieu Vineyard winemaker André Tchelistcheff, has been a consultant at Pindar.

The tasting room, in a century-old barn, is open daily, from 11 a.m. to 6 p.m. and is understandably very popular. The informative, detailed tours of the winery are at noon, 2 p.m. and 4 p.m.

Pugliese Vineyards

Route 25, Cutchogue
631-734-4057; 631-734-5668 (fax)

Pugliese Vineyards is a small, family-run winery, full of concentrated wines, sparklers and heart.

Ralph and Pat Pugliese started their winery in 1980. Before that, Ralph led a plasterers union. His family produced wine in Italy, and he began making it in Brooklyn.

Their Cutchogue acreage totals 30. Pugliese grows chardonnay, merlot, cabernet sauvignon and some sangiovese. The Puglieses also grew Long Island's lone stretch of zinfandel. Peter Pugliese, Ralph and Pat's son, is the winemaker. He creates sturdy reds, fruity chardonnays, a line of attractive sparkling wines, dessert wines and fortified wines. A Pugliese Port is high-octane, cold-

ESTATE BOTTLED
1997

Pugliese Vineyards Champagne

Blanc de Blanc Brut

NORTH FORK OF LONG ISLAND

GROWN, PRODUCED AND BOTTLED BY
PUGLIESE VINEYARDS, INC.
CUTCHOGUE, LONG ISLAND, NEW YORK
ALC. 11.5% BY VOLUME CONTAINS SULFITES

750mL

weather drinking.

And this is the only winery on Long Island where you'll locate a sparkling merlot, which the Puglieses call "red Champagne."

Trying something new, whether this red wine or the zinfandel, reflects the Pugliese approach. Pugliese generally is at its best with bubbles, which suits the style of the operation. The image is countrified and fun, from the ducks drifting by on the nearby pond to the old gas pump in front of the building. Pugliese is devoid of pretense and the wines reflect that.

In the tasting room, you may see Pat Pugliese decorating and personalizing bottles by hand.

The tasting room is open from 10:30 a.m. to 6 p.m. on weekends, and to 5 p.m. on weekdays. There are no tours. The gift shop includes Ralph Pugliese Jr.'s evocative landscape photography.

Raphael

Main Road (Route 25), Peconic
631-765-1100
www.raphaelwine.com

No winery on the East End has made so big an impression as Raphael before even opening a door or releasing a wine.

Raphael is the project of Ronkonkoma builder John Petrocelli, whose experience must include churches because the winery under construction has an inspired look. It's a generally Mediterranean style, and on Route

25, it certainly stands out. The estate is named in honor of Petrocelli's father. The winery was visited while under construction. It's a combination of very current technology and very traditional style.

The goal of Petrocelli and winemaker Richard Olsen-Harbich, a veteran of Long Island wineries, is to produce one wine: a merlot-based red that will be called Raphael, just as the crus of Bordeaux are named for their estates instead of the grape variety. Paul Pontallier, general manager of Chateau Margaux, a top cru Bordeaux, is a consultant at Raphael.

In addition to merlot, the 42 acres of Raphael vineyards grow small amounts of cabernet franc, malbec and petit verdot, which often are used in Bordeaux blends. The hand-picked grapes eventually should yield 10,000 cases annually, said Olsen-Harbich.

Release of the 1997 estate-bottled Raphael is scheduled for June 2001, as is the opening of the winery.

Schneider Vineyards

2248 Roanoke Ave., Riverhead
631-727-3334; 631-727-3242 (fax)
www.schneidervineyards.com

Schneider Vineyards is a winery in the works.
It started as perhaps Long Island's most unusual wine operation. Bruce and Christiane Baker Schneider had no vineyard and no winery. They began as local vintners, selecting old-vine grapes from North Fork producers. The wines were made at Bedell Cellars and Palmer Vineyards.

The Schneiders purchased 22 acres in Riverhead last year for their estate vineyard. Seven acres have been

planted. The Schneiders' emphasis, as it has been all along, is cabernet franc. They expect 10 acres of the vineyard will be cabernet franc, five merlot, 1.5 each malbec and cabernet sauvignon, and one acre petit verdot.

Bruce is from the third generation of a family of importers, and he has done apprenticeships in the vineyards of Burgundy. The couple had considered starting their enterprise in Europe or California before coming to the North Fork in 1992. Their cabernet franc campaign began with the 1994 vintage. The wines generally have been very good.

In addition to the Schneider label, they are responsible for the current-release blends Potato Barn White and Potato Barn Red. These are more casual wines to be enjoyed, as they say, with "the spud of your choice."

The Schneiders are planning a high-end, proprietary blend that will be 60 percent to 70 percent cabernet franc, from grapes grown in the new vineyard, which is the most westerly on the East End. They're a few years away from that. But the couple expects their tasting room, in a converted potato barn, to open in summer 2001.

Ternhaven Cellars

331 Front St., Greenport
631-477-8737

The sign outside Ternhaven Cellars announces that the next winery along the way is in France. This is definitely the east end of Long Island wine country.

Owner Harold W. Watts is the winemaker. He taught public policy at Columbia University for 22 years. Watts, who was raised on a farm in Oregon, also was making wine in his apartment.

These days, Ternhaven Cellars produces about 700 cases of wine annually. The professor emeritus' lead wine is called Claret d'Alvah, a red blend that's mostly merlot. Watts started making the wines with the 1997 vintage. Earlier, they were produced by Russell Hearn at Pellegrini Vineyards.

Watts came to New York in 1976 from the University of Wisconsin. En route, he saw wines being made in the middle of Pennsylvania. Watts began making wine at his home a decade later. First, he purchased grapes for that wine.

Then, he grew them in Cutchogue, where Ternhaven's five-acre vineyard is located. Local restrictions barred him from opening the winery in Cutchogue, where Ternhaven's size fell short of the minimum acreage required. So, Watts set up the winery in downtown Greenport, where it's one of the main attractions along a reborn Front Street.

Ternhaven's aim is to make Bordeaux-style reds. No white wines are planned. In addition to Claret d'Alvah, Watts makes merlot, cabernet sauvignon and a rosé that includes Finger Lakes region grapes.

The winery and tasting room are open Friday, Saturday and Sunday, from 11 a.m. to 5 p.m., and later in summer. Tours are available. Watts said a tour "takes about four minutes."

Wölffer Estate

139 Sagg Rd., Sagaponack
631-537-5106; 631-537-5107 (fax)
www.wolffer.com

Whether you see it as a grand Tuscan farmhouse or a sun-splashed, stuccoed villa, Wölffer Estate's Sagaponack chateau is among the most European and most opulent of Long Island's wineries.

The estate is venture capitalist Christian Wölffer's enterprise, established in 1987 on what had been a potato field. Wölffer's career has taken him into investment banking and real estate. He has a varied one here alone.

Wölffer

1998
The Hamptons, Long Island
ESTATE SELECTION
MERLOT

ESTATE BOTTLED BY SAGPOND VINEYARDS
SAGAPONACK, NEW YORK, USA • ALC. 13% BY VOL. • 750 ML

Wölffer's South Fork land is about 170 acres. Wölffer
Estate accounts for 55. Until 1997, the wine-producing
wing was called Sagpond Vineyards. While the vineyards
keep the name, the wines are Wölffer.

The Sagaponack property is home to Sagpond Stables,
for horse breeding, boarding, schooling and riding. Wölffer
Estate Farms maintains a farm stand on Montauk Highway.
Sagpond Farmstead Cheese is produced on the premises.
It's a tasty, Swiss-style cheese that will remind you of a
mild, nutty Emmentaler. Wölffer also sells vintage-dated
verjus, made with chardonnay grape juice. Verjus is a less
tart alternative to vinegar and very versatile for cooking.

Roman Roth has been the winemaker at Wölffer since
1992. His wines total about 9,000 cases annually.

The varieties include four levels of merlot, topped by
the estate selection label; several chardonnays, including
a dessert wine; cabernet franc; a dry rosé; and a brut-
style sparkling wine. He also has produced vivid pinot
noir with grapes from a Manorville vineyard.

The winery is open daily, from 11 a.m. to 5 p.m. Tours
are by appointment.

Chardonnay on the vine.

Chapter 3

A Glass of White Wine

Chardonnay and beyond

White wines range in color from pale straw to deep gold, and in character from steely and dry to honeyed and sweet. Each grape variety yields a very different wine. And, in some cases, more than one. These grapes actually are green or yellow, and sometimes shades in-between. You can make white wine from red wine grapes, too. The pigment resides in the skin of the grape, not the juice.

Here's a look at the main white grape varieties grown on

Long Island, and reviews of selected wines made from them.

The grape varieties discussed include chardonnay, chenin blanc, gewürztraminer, pinot blanc, pinot gris, riesling, sauvignon blanc, semillon and viognier. There is also a section devoted to white blends.

As is the case throughout this book, the prices accompanying the reviews generally are those at the time of the wine's release and are subject to change.

Chardonnay

Chardonnay, to many, is synonymous with "a glass of white wine." It leads any report on white wine grapes, just as cabernet sauvignon does for the reds.

The popularity of the grape is worldwide and takes in consumers, growers and winemakers. Chardonnay has a short growing season and does well in cooler climates and exacting soils.

Chardonnay yields are high. And the grape has ample versatility. Winemakers can style chardonnay in many ways. More than any other white wine grape, it has compatibility with oak. Barrel-fermented chardonnays typically are full-bodied. Chardonnays fermented in steel tanks are crisper and cleaner.

The grape reaches its refined zenith in Burgundy, where Chablis, Corton-Charlemagne, Meursault and Montrachet are among its wines, as well as the popular Pouilly-Fuissé. Chardonnay is essential in Champagne, the Loire Valley, Friuli and Trentino in northern Italy and Australia.

Chardonnay is also revered in California, especially in wines of producers such as Kistler, Marcassin, Peter Michael, Robert Talbott and Steele; in regions including Carneros and the Russian River Valley.

On Long Island, it's by far the most widely planted grape. In sales, it's number one, too.

1998 Banfi Old Brookville Chardonnay
True to its annual style, the wine is round, buttery, easy drinking. You'll detect a trace of apple. The wine is very good with food. There's no 1999 vintage. The 2000 chardonnay will be made in Mattituck instead of upstate Hammondsport. $12.

1997 Banfi Old Brookville Chardonnay
Buttery, appealing and up-

front, it's one of the better chardonnays from the Nassau County vineyard. $12.

1997 Bedell Chardonnay Reserve

Mouth-filling, creamy and elegant, the wine displays a distinctive richness and style. $15.

1996 Bedell Chardonnay Reserve

Smooth and attractive. The wine was fermented and aged in French oak and has the expected butteriness, and a hint of honeysuckle. $15.

1996 Bedell Chardonnay

Up-front with tropical fruit, mainly pineapple. An easygoing white that pairs well with mild-flavored finfish. $10.

1995 Bedell Chardonnay Reserve

Deftly balanced and refined. The fruitiness has come to the fore. Understated and very attractive. $15.

1995 Bedell Chardonnay

Fermented primarily in steel, it's a crisp and fruity number with considerable character. $12.

1994 Bedell Chardonnay Reserve

It remains appealing. Full-bodied, showing off more vanilla and butterscotch. But the hints of pear are still there. Still drinking very well. $16.

1994 Bedell Chardonnay

The tank-fermented "silver label" chardonnay is good both for sipping and with a light meal. But fading. $12.

1993 Bedell Chardonnay Reserve

The structure is good and the flavors surprisingly vibrant. The wine has some time left. $15.

1993 Bedell Chardonnay

Satisfying, if you can find it. But best days are gone. $12.

1992 Bedell Chardonnay Reserve

Just past its prime now, but balanced and elegant with a finish that continues. $15.

1992 Bedell Chardonnay

Faded elegance, but worth trying, if you can find it, to see how local chardonnays last. $12.

1997 Bidwell Barrel Fermented Chardonnay

Tropical flavors run through the wine. The oak makes its mark with a toasty rush. It was aged a bit on the yeast lees. Supple and balanced. $15.

1996 Bidwell Barrel Fermented Chardonnay

Light oak and tropical flavors remain the primary characteristics of this balanced wine. $15.

1994 Bidwell Barrel Fermented Chardonnay
Toasty, with traces of pear and more of vanilla. But on the light side and past prime time. $16.

1993 Bidwell Reserve Chardonnay
Fairly light and uncomplicated. Getting old. $15.

1999 Channing Daughters Brick Kiln Chardonnay
Respectable varietal character, with hints of apple. A barrel-fermented, medium-bodied wine. $17.

1999 Channing Daughters Scuttlehole Chardonnay
Straightforward, steel-fermented production, with respectable acidity. $13.

1998 Channing Daughters Brick Kiln Chardonnay
Minerally, buttery, toasty. A spirited, medium-bodied wine with more complexity than the earlier vintage. Lots of apple and citrus. $15.

1998 Channing Daughters Scuttlehole Chardonnay
Lemon and apple notes in this chardonnay, with hints of spice, too. $13.

1997 Channing Daughters Brick Kiln Chardonnay
The first white released by the winery. Citric and refreshing. The wine was made by Channing Daughters at Peconic Bay Winery. $17.

1998 Corey Creek Reserve Chardonnay
Full-bodied, buttery and yeasty, with more than a suggestion of vanilla and oak. Burgundian style. $17.

1998 Corey Creek Chardonnay
Slightly minerally, refreshing, crisp, fruit-loaded and versatile with food. Fermented in steel and oak. $14.

1997 Corey Creek Reserve Chardonnay
Toasty and balanced, this is a first-rate chardonnay that continues to drink well. There are hints of spice, too. A fine food wine. $15.

1997 Corey Creek Chardonnay
Elegantly balanced and very good. It has the personality of a Chablis. Mineral notes, fine acidity. $14.

1996 Corey Creek Chardonnay
Very fruity and balanced. It's a textbook wine to have with your seafood dinner. $11.

1995 Corey Creek Reserve Chardonnay
Bright and tasty, with excellent fruit and just enough oak. $16.

**1995 Corey Creek
Chardonnay**
Balanced, fruity, with some
mineral notes. $14.

**1994 Corey Creek
Reserve Chardonnay**
Full-bodied and buttery. An
appetizing wine that doesn't
overdo the oak. Good fruit and
a long finish. Made at Palmer
Vineyards. $16.

**1994 Corey Creek
Chardonnay**
Medium-bodied, good fruit and
balance. But slowly on the way
out. $13.

**1997 Duck Walk
Chardonnay Reserve**
Buttery and balanced, full, with
nuances of tropical fruit. $13.

1997 Duck Walk Chardonnay
Pear and vanilla notes mark this
workmanlike chardonnay, which
benefited from some oak. $9.

**1995 Duck Walk
Chardonnay Reserve**
Good fruit, pretty smooth. $13.

1995 Duck Walk Chardonnay
Citrusy. But that's it. $10.

**1994 Duck Walk
Chardonnay Reserve**
User-friendly chardonnay that
lightens up the reserve category. Some tropical notes. Made
with North Fork grapes. $13.

1994 Duck Walk Chardonnay
Herbal, modest, about done. $9.

1995 Dzugas Chardonnay
A clean opening act. The sweet
label is an added smile. $12.

1999 Gristina Chardonnay
Creamy, balanced, toasty, with
traces of orange peel. $20.

**1998 Gristina
Andy's Field Chardonnay**
Very ripe and neatly styled,
silky, with pear notes and a
long finish. Medium-bodied,
with traces of spice. $40.

1998 Gristina Chardonnay
Citrus notes sound in this
fruity chardonnay. $20.

**1997 Gristina
Andy's Field Chardonnay**
Vanilla and honey highlight the
creamy, excellent chardonnay,
which deftly balances the fruit
and the oak. $22.

**1995 Gristina
Andy's Field Chardonnay**
Outstanding chardonnay.
Creamy, rich, toasty. It has
matured nicely, with pear and
apple overtones. Elegant all
around, with a long finish. $22.

1995 Gristina Chardonnay
Very good, with suggestions of
spice and pear. Not a bad sipper. $14.

1994 Gristina Chardonnay
Light, with fine acidity and a zesty flavor that has a touch of citrus to it. Good mouth-feel. $14.

**1993 Gristina
Andy's Field Chardonnay**
It had depth at the outset and continues to drink well. Full-bodied and refined, with traces of vanilla, pear. Smoky qualities, too. $19.

1993 Gristina Chardonnay
Concentrated, slightly citric, aromatic. Unlikely to get any better than it is now. $14.

**1998 Hargrave
Chardonnay Reserve**
Toasty, with good varietal character and mouth-feel. An able advocate for the vintage. Buttery, but not too much. $18.

1998 Hargrave Chardonnay
Citrus and vanilla combine in this fresh, clean wine. $13.

**Hargrave
Chardonette**
Crisp and forward, this is a well-priced introduction to local chardonnays. It has a Gallic accent. $7.

**1997 Hargrave
Chardonnay Reserve**
Loaded with fruit. Ripe, full and fine, with excellent varietal character and toasty notes. $16.

**1995 Hargrave Lattice Label
Chardonnay**
When released, an excellent, harmonious chardonnay, plump and toasty, with aspects of vanilla and pear. It's textbook stuff. $15.

**1994 Hargrave Lattice Label
Chardonnay**
Not as opulent as the immediately preceding and succeeding wines. Fading. $15.

**1993 Hargrave Lattice Label
Chardonnay**
A reserve chardonnay with finesse, the wine has a delightful aroma and varietal character par excellence. Among the leading wines from Hargrave. $20.

1993 Hargrave Chardonnay
More soothing than assertive in its varietal character. The wine is good company for light dishes. But don't expect it to age much more. $15.

**1998 Jamesport Cox Lane
Chardonnay**
Hints of dried fruit, some tropical accents. Satisfying. $14.

**1997 Jamesport Cox Lane
Chardonnay**
Smooth, with seven months spent in French oak. You'll detect a whiff of peach and the trademark vanilla. $15.

1997 Jamesport Natural Selection Chardonnay
Ripe and full-bodied, with traces of spice and fine varietal character. $18.

1996 Jamesport Chardonnay
Satisfactory. $10.

1995 Jamesport Cox Lane Chardonnay
Medium-bodied with minerally, citrusy notes. Tank-fermented and barrel-aged. Not too complicated. $13.

1995 Jamesport Three Barrel Chardonnay
Good chardonnay with traces of tropical fruit. Still tasty. $16.

1993 Jamesport Cox Lane Chardonnay
Past prime. $13.

1993 Jamesport Three Barrel Chardonnay
Still has some modest appeal. $18.

1998 Laurel Lake Reserve Chardonnay
More perched than balanced. $15.

1997 Laurel Lake Reserve Chardonnay
Among the better wines to carry the Laurel Lake label. The chardonnay has traces of vanilla, chestnut, pear and spice. $15.

1996 Laurel Lake Chardonnay
Lean sipper. $9.

1995 Laurel Lake Chardonnay
Good, with some depth. $15.

1994 Laurel Lake Chardonnay
Faded. $15.

1998 Lenz Barrel Fermented Chardonnay
A winning white that compares favorably with its Burgundy relatives. It has depth, very good fruit and a long finish. Lenz's "gold label" chardonnay. $25.

1998 Lenz Vineyard Selection Chardonnay
Fruity, attractive and sure to be consumed quickly. Also very much like a Burgundy, but a lighter one. The "white label" chardonnay. $11.

1997 Lenz Barrel Fermented Chardonnay
From 19-year-old vines, with lots of ripe grapes. Concentrated and showing its many virtues young. $25.

1997 Lenz Silver Label Chardonnay
Between the "gold" and the "white" is this new entry, lighter than the former and fuller than the latter. Moderation as a virtue. $15.

**1997 Lenz Vineyard
Selection Chardonnay**
Burgundian chardonnay, fresh,
open, crisp and fruity. $10.

**1996 Lenz Barrel
Fermented Chardonnay**
Toasty, reductive, yeasty, appley
and quite rich. The grapes
must have thrived during the
cooler season. May last longer
than the '97. $25.

**1996 Lenz Vineyard
Selection Chardonnay**
A classy, very appealing
chardonnay. Definitely one of
the better chardonnays from
this vintage; better than most
reserves. $10.

**1995 Lenz Barrel
Fermented Chardonnay**
Rich and reliable, with a
Francophile style. Reductive,
concentrated, Burgundian, with
traces of peach, apricot, some
nuttiness. $25.

**1995 Lenz Vineyard
Selection Chardonnay**
Lighter, with good varietal
character, vanilla notes. Clean
and harmonious. A bread-and-
butter food wine. $10.

**1994 Lenz Barrel
Fermented Chardonnay**
Balances oak and fruit with
flair. A reminder of Meursault.
$25.

**1994 Lenz Vineyard
Selection Chardonnay**
Lots of pear, some citrus.
Finished with a bit of pinot
blanc. $10.

**1993 Lenz Barrel
Fermented Chardonnay**
Generous and satisfying. The
wine is forthright with oak and
pear, creamy and buttery. Aging
potential fulfilled. $20.

**1993 Lenz Vineyard
Selection Chardonnay**
Fruity and flavor-packed, with
fine acidity and a pleasing finish. Trademark chardonnay. $11.

1999 Lieb Chardonnay
Forward and fruity chardonnay.
Very good with seafood. Made
at Paumanok Vineyards. $15.

**1999 Loughlin
Chardonnay Reserve**
Light, with a bit of citrus. Made
at Peconic Bay Winery. $12.

1995 Loughlin Chardonnay
Satisfactory varietal character,
crisp and good. Also made at
Peconic Bay. $11.

**1998 Macari
Chardonnay Reserve**
Very good fruit, with a tropical
accent and undertones of oak.
$19.

**1998 Macari
Estate Chardonnay**
Clean and refreshing, fruity

and crisp. Traces of apple. $15.

1997 Macari Barrel Fermented Chardonnay
The winery's most notable white, and still the best, with a big bouquet and mouth-filling style. $19.

1997 Macari Chardonnay Reserve
Round, with pear notes. Dry. $14.

1996 Macari Barrel Fermented Chardonnay
Buttery notes, toasty character, a hint of citrus. $14.

1999 Martha Clara Reserve Chardonnay
The first reserve from this vineyard, with very good body and varietal character. Barrel-fermented and barrel-aged. $17.

1999 Martha Clara Chardonnay
Medium-bodied, barrel-fermented and aged in steel. Crisp, fruit-forward and yeasty. $10.

1998 Osprey's Dominion Reserve Chardonnay
Full-bodied, food-friendly, barrel-fermented wine. Traces of vanilla and oak. Tropical fruit and appley notes, too. $22.

1998 Osprey's Dominion Chardonnay
Partly barrel-fermented and refreshing. It has a suggestion of tropical fruit, with apricot-peach notes. Good sipper. $12.

1997 Osprey's Dominion Reserve Chardonnay
Among the best whites made at Osprey, with lots of tropical fruit and citrusy character. Round, easygoing for a reserve. $22.

1997 Osprey's Dominion Chardonnay
Crisp, with tropical fruit notes. $13.

1996 Osprey's Dominion Chardonnay
Melon and pear notes punctuate this respectable, barrel-fermented chardonnay. $13.

1995 Osprey's Dominion Chardonnay
Notes of pear play through this satisfying white, which has oaky nuances. $13.

Osprey's Dominion Regina Maris Chardonnay
Crisp and to the point, with tropical fruit touches and some toastiness. $8.

Osprey's Dominion Bayman's Harvest
Light, blunt, with hints of melon. $8.

1998 Palmer Reserve Chardonnay
Another dependable reserve, with buttery notes and suggestions of pear, apple and citrus. $15.

1998 Palmer Estate Chardonnay
Good acidity and an easygoing style are the heart of this clean, food-friendly wine, with lemon and apple threading through. $12.

1997 Palmer Reserve Chardonnay
Full, ripe, first-rate wine with a near-ideal balance of fruit, oak and acidity. The winery's star of recent vintages. Butterscotch notes, tropical fruit. Long finish. $15.

1997 Palmer Estate Chardonnay
Crisp, lemony and refreshing, with good, up-front fruit. $12.

1996 Palmer Barrel Fermented Chardonnay
Lacks the fullness of the '95, but refreshing, with light oak and high acidity. $15.

1996 Palmer Estate Chardonnay
Lively, with lemony flavors and a minerally quality. Very Californian, Central Coast variety. $12.

1995 Palmer Barrel Fermented Chardonnay
The kind of wine you'll always associate with this winery. Pear notes, toasty oak. Buttery and first-rate. $17.

1995 Palmer Estate Chardonnay
Fruity and snappy, with hints of mango and pineapple. But not long to go. $12.

1994 Palmer Barrel Fermented Chardonnay
Yeasty, heady with pear and apple. Butterscotch notes. Smooth. $15.

1993 Palmer Barrel Fermented Chardonnay
Well-developed, toasty and rich, with a suggestion of the lees. Mouth-filling. The wine has developed with style. $15.

1999 Paumanok Barrel Fermented Chardonnay
Fruity, flavorful varietal, and on the lighter side. Tasted early. $17.

1998 Paumanok Barrel Fermented Chardonnay
Mouth-filling, with lots of oak, yeastiness, earthiness. The wine has character and will have a longer life than most local chardonnays. Excellent with rich dishes. $17.

1997 Paumanok Barrel Fermented Chardonnay
Buttery and first-rate. Mouth-filling, with superior fruit and varietal character. It has relatives in Burgundy, not California. Classic food wine. $17.

**1995 Paumanok Grand
Vintage Chardonnay**
Penetrating, rich and delightful,
with overtones of spice and
enough complexity to make you
wish you had a case or two.
Creamy, harmonious and supple, with hints of tropical fruit.
Made from a single vineyard
bloc and free-run juice, aged in
new French oak. Many plea-
sures. Still exceptional. $24.

**1995 Paumanok Barrel
Fermented Chardonnay**
Ripe and juicy, with loads of
terrific fruit. Very smooth. $17.

**1994 Paumanok Barrel
Fermented Chardonnay**
Lean, with a hint of oak. $15.

**Paumanok Festival
Chardonnay**
Light, refreshing party wine.
$10.

**1999 Peconic Bay
La Barrique Chardonnay**
Barrel-fermented in French
oak. The wine has considerable
finesse at an early age, with a
yeasty touch. More balanced
style than earlier Peconic Bay
chardonnays. $17.

**1998 Peconic Bay
Chardonnay**
Lean. $11.

**1998 Peconic Bay
Sandy Hill Chardonnay**
Ripe fruit, very oaky. $16.

**1996 Peconic Bay
Sandy Hill Chardonnay**
Flavorful, with citrus and
spice. But tiring. $22.

**1995 Peconic Bay
Sandy Hill Chardonnay**
Balanced, with traces of melon
and more than a hint of oak.
$22.

**1995 Peconic Bay
Rolling Ridge Chardonnay**
Toast, butterscotch notes. The
successor to the winery's reserve. Satisfying with food. $18.

**1995 Peconic Bay
Chardonnay**
Green apple quality. Lean. $12.

**1999 Pellegrini East End
Select Chardonnay**
The youngster in the reper-
toire. Fruity and light. $9.

**1998 Pellegrini Vintner's
Pride Chardonnay**
Excellent mouth-feel and fruitiness are the hallmarks here. A
round, satisfying white that
calls for richer seafood, perhaps cream sauce. $23.

1998 Pellegrini Chardonnay
Notes of pear and apple mark
this enjoyable, creamy
chardonnay. $13.

**1997 Pellegrini Vintner's
Pride Chardonnay**
Top-of-the-line chardonnay
from this producer. Much fruit:
pear, lemon. Buttery notes. $23.

1997 Pellegrini Chardonnay
Fruity and aromatic, with suggestions of grapefruit. It has a
creamy, lush quality, from 11
months' barrel-aging. $13.

1996 Pellegrini Chardonnay
Short on fruit. $13.

**1995 Pellegrini Vintner's
Pride Chardonnay**
Big, creamy, polished chardonnay. Round, smooth, with
aspects of ripe pear and hazelnut, a fine hint of vanilla and a
grand finish. $23.

1995 Pellegrini Chardonnay
Crisp, balanced, with hints of
apple and pear. $13.

**1994 Pellegrini Vintner's
Pride Chardonnay**
Much pear, modest oak from 18
months in the barrel. A fine
chardonnay. $20.

1994 Pellegrini Chardonnay
Tropical fruit notes and some
earthiness. $15.

**1998 Pindar Peacock Label
Chardonnay**
Refreshing, crisp, easygoing
wine that was 20 percent barrel-fermented. $9.

**1998 Pindar
Reserve Chardonnay**
The barrel-fermented wine spent
a year in French oak. Traces of
apple. Long finish. $13.

**1998 Pindar Sunflower
Chardonnay**
Slightly less oaky than the
familiar Sunflower thanks to
the ripeness of the '98 fruit.
Some tropical fruit nuances.
Still the winery's resident
Californian. $17.

**1997 Pindar Peacock Label
Chardonnay**
Up-front, fresh, with lively
acidity. $9.

**1997 Pindar
Reserve Chardonnay**
Full-bodied, fruity, balanced,
open and a trifle toasty. $13.

**1997 Pindar
Sunflower Chardonnay**
The oaky style that has long
defined this wine is in true
form here. There's good fruit
and a tropical accent, too. $16.

**1996 Pindar Peacock Label
Chardonnay**
Pear and tropical fruit notes in
this crisp, light wine. $11.

**1996 Pindar
Reserve Chardonnay**
Oaky, with light butterscotch
notes. A lean reserve. $16.

1995 Pindar
Reserve Chardonnay
Ripe and toasty, with fine balance and confident style. Lobster wine. $15.

1998 Pugliese
Chardonnay Reserve
Some pear and apple greet you from this blunt, dry barrel-fermented production. $13.

Pugliese Chardonnay Gold
Soft, versatile with food. $10.

1997 Pugliese
Chardonnay Reserve
A bit lemony and appley. Soft and not very dry. $13.

1995 Pugliese
Chardonnay Reserve
Dry, barrel-fermented, with a citrusy finish. $13.

1998 Schneider Chardonnay
Lively and balanced, with good fruit. Melon notes. Not as creamy as the '97. $19.

1997 Schneider Chardonnay
Clean, fresh, medium-bodied, creamy, with lots of fruit. Oak is more a backdrop than an assertive partner. Made for Schneider at Palmer Vineyards. $19.

1998 SilverStone
Chardonnay
The second installment of California winemaker and Long Island veteran Dan Kleck's expatriate wine, made with his successor, Tom Drozd, long-distance at Palmer Vineyards. Satisfying. $18.

1997 SilverStone
Chardonnay
A fruity chardonnay made at Palmer Vineyards from Palmer and Lieb Vineyards fruit. $18.

1998 Wölffer
Reserve Chardonnay
Buttery, satisfying, with light toasty notes. Tasted early. $18.

1998 Wölffer La Ferme
Martin Chardonnay
Crisp, refreshing and spurred by lemon and apple accents. Refreshing. And a complement for spicy foods and shellfish. $13.

1997 Wölffer Estate
Selection Chardonnay
Elegant, balanced and buttery, with fine fruit, toastiness and most of the qualities that make for a first-class Long Island chardonnay. $28.

1997 Wölffer
Reserve Chardonnay
Clean finish, crisper style and more minerally than the Estate Selection. Very flinty, trés French. $18.

1997 Wölffer Chardonnay
Echoes the bright and light La Ferme Martin. A trifle tart. $13.

**1996 Wölffer
Reserve Chardonnay**
Concentrated and very satisfying big brother to the regular bottling. Whatever problems reds had in '96, they didn't harm the whites, especially this one. $17.

1996 Wölffer Chardonnay
Fruity chardonnay, tropical variety, with some time left on the clock. Creamy and round. $13.

**1995 Wölffer Estate
Selection Chardonnay**
Ample spice, fruit and a pronounced affection for oak, which has mellowed beautifully over time. Pears and honey come to mind. Very ripe, very smooth, with considerable life. $25.

**1995 Wölffer
Reserve Chardonnay**
Lemony flavor makes an appearance in this bright, yeasty, flinty wine, which has depth and character, plus a shot of oak. $15.

**1995 Wölffer La Ferme
Martin Chardonnay**
Crisp and lemony. Summertime wine. $13.

**1994 Wölffer Estate
Selection Chardonnay**
Concentrated, multi-dimensional chardonnay with a delicate balance of fruit and oak. Burgundy alert. $25.

**1994 Wölffer
Reserve Chardonnay**
Dry and velvety, with a lemony, appley accent, subtle earthiness. $15.

**1993 Wölffer
Reserve Chardonnay**
Ripe fruit, with hints of apple, fig and lemon. Yeasty, with oak notes. Getting on. $15.

Chenin Blanc

Chenin blanc is the grape of the Loire Valley, the Touraine and Anjou, as well as South Africa, where it's often called steen. Chenin blanc has high acidity and is blended into wines still and sparkling, sweet and dry. But think mainly of Vouvray and Saumur.

The grape leads two happy lives. The young wines are immediate gratification, floral, slightly sweet and light. Chenin also is the source of excellent late-harvest dessert wines in France. That high acidity leads to wines capable of long lives.

Locally, only Paumanok Vineyards has released chenin blanc.

2000 Paumanok Chenin Blanc
The 2000 vintage provided a fruity, forward, instantly enjoyable chenin, with hints of citrus. Try it with shellfish. $15.

1999 Paumanok Chenin Blanc
Dry and very attractive. A real taste of the Loire on the East End. $15.

1998 Paumanok Chenin Blanc
A soft white with notes of grapefruit, but less acidity than in previous years. Appealing, though getting old. $14.

1997 Paumanok Chenin Blanc
Hate to see you go. $14.

Gewürztraminer

Spicy, floral, pungent and intensely fragrant, gewürztraminer is a very recognizable wine.

The grape can be made into a fruity or dry wine, or a viscous dessert wine. It has a pink cast, and the wines made from gewürztraminer can be more golden than other whites.

Gewürztraminer does best in Alsace, but also is grown in the Alto Adige of Italy, where it may have originated, Eastern Europe and in parts of California and the Pacific Northwest. It has met with some success on the East End. Cooler weather is its companion.

The dry gewürztraminers should be consumed early. The sweet wines have a longer life.

1998 Bedell Gewürztraminer
The dry variety, light and very good, with rose notes. It tastes right with Indian and Chinese cuisine. $13.

1995 Bedell Gewürztraminer
A rose-petal aroma highlights this wine, which doesn't overdo the spice. $10.

1999 Martha Clara Gewürztraminer
Litchis and an undercurrent of spice run through this neatly balanced, dry wine that contains 10 percent riesling. Sample it with Asian fare. $16.

1998 Lenz Gewürztraminer
The fruit comes forward in this gewürztraminer, which down-

plays the house's trademark spicy qualities. Very refreshing and versatile. $12.

1997 Lenz Estate Gewürztraminer
An excellent gewürztraminer, with vibrant acidity and textbook Alsatian style. $12.

1994 Lenz Gewürztraminer
A spirited gewürztraminer that's in its pretty sunset. $11.

1993 Lenz Gewürztraminer
Old for a local gewürztraminer, but it continues to have spirited fruit and a disarming Alsatian charm. $20.

1999 Palmer Gewürztraminer
Very good, with suggestions of rose, litchi. Dry, Alsatian style. On a par with the '97 and preferable to the '98. $15.

1998 Palmer Gewürztraminer
Spicy and aromatic, with litchi and grapefruit notes. $15.

1997 Palmer Gewürztraminer
Grapefruit and litchis thread through this very fragrant, fruit-driven wine. $15.

1996 Palmer Gewürztraminer
Lighter, sweeter than the '95. $15.

Pinot Blanc

France, Germany and Italy are among the homes for pinot blanc. For contrast, compare one from the Alto Adige with an Alsatian, then throw a Californian into the contest.

The grape may be used in blending. But it's a brisk, lively varietal, acidic and not overpowering in flavor. Accordingly, very versatile.

The dry wines never reach the complexity of chardonnay or have the character of riesling, but they're fresh and ideal in summer. The East End has produced a few winners that match neatly with seafood.

1999 Hargrave Pinot Blanc
Dry and summery, this is a clean and satisfying white that's right with light finfish or pastas. $10.

1998 Hargrave Pinot Blanc
Light, attractive and as much northern Italian as it is Alsatian. Clean and fruity. $10.

1995 Hargrave Pinot Blanc
Alsatian in style, with fine acidity, refreshing character. $10.

1995 Lenz Pinot Blanc
Dry, minerally, lean, expressive, with a hint of hazelnut. $11.

1994 Lenz Pinot Blanc
Very dry, breezy and clean, with

a touch of citrus and nuances of tropical fruit. $11.

1993 Lenz Pinot Blanc
Memorable pinot, dry and delightful when released. But past peak. $13.

1998 Lieb Pinot Blanc
Crisp, inviting and summery, this is the first pinot blanc under the label of a family whose vineyard has provided others with excellent fruit. Brisk. Made at Macari Vineyards. $15.

1998 Macari Pinot Blanc
Frisky and summery. The wine works as an aperitif or with seafood. $12.

1998 Palmer Estate Pinot Blanc
The wine contains a little chardonnay that helps broaden the palate. Clean, with more crispness than fruit. $10.

1997 Palmer Lieb Vineyard Pinot Blanc
Refreshing and pleasingly acidic on release, with traces of melon and vanilla. An aperitif, too. Little time left. $13.

1996 Palmer Lieb Vineyard Pinot Blanc
Very good fruit and a clean, crisp refresher when released. Holding on. $13.

1996 Palmer Estate Pinot Blanc
Crisp, uncomplicated, good. $10.

Pinot Gris

Pinot grigio is ordered so often you'd think it's chardonnay's number one challenger.

The Italian wines made with the grape are light, occasionally thin and very easy to drink. Alsatian pinot gris typically has more body and character. And there are honeyed pinots. The grape also is called petit gris, pinot beurot and rulander.

Pinot gris isn't planted widely in the United States. Look to Oregon. So far, only a couple of them have been made on Long Island. But it's a grape with enough versatility to stick around.

1998 Duck Walk Pinot Gris
A South Fork spin on pinot grigio. Has an Oregon accent. Easygoing with lots of foods. $15.

1998 Lenz Pinot Gris
Lenz fashioned the pinot gris from North Fork grapes. It's a fat Alsatian in style and very refreshing. $20.

Riesling

The great grape of Germany has many styles. It has lost to chardonnay in popularity, but rieslings can be extraordinary wines, complex and delightful. This sturdy vine has no problem with cooler climates. In Alsace, rieslings are made dry; in Germany, they're fruitier and more aromatic, headquartered in the Rheingau. As a late-harvest wine, riesling reaches remarkable sweetness.

For Alsatian riesling, try the wines of Hugel, Trimbach and Zind-Humbrecht; for German, Klaus Neckerauer, Kurt Darting and Werle.

Riesling's qualities go from apple and peach to orange peel when the wine is dry. Ice wines made from riesling often offer traces of citrus and pineapple. When the noble rot botrytis cinerea strikes, the result is lush, honeyed sometimes nutty, with the intensity of dried fruit.

You'll see riesling labeled Johannisberg riesling and white riesling, especially in the United States. In an era of chardonnay madness, it's a lovely alternative.

1999 Bidwell White Riesling
Fruity, off-dry and an easygoing, local introduction to the varietal. $10.

**1996 Bidwell
Dry White Riesling**
Crisp and good, with tasty fruit. Serve not too chilled. $13.

1996 Bidwell White Riesling
Fresh and unpretentious, with suggestion of pineapple. Chill it. $10.

**1998 Channing Perrine
Oregon Road Dry Riesling**
Zesty wine with mineral notes. The winery's first from these old vines on the North Fork. Very good. $13.

**1997 Channing Perrine
Rolling Ridge Dry Riesling**
Dry and refreshing, with pleasing varietal character. $12.

1997 Jamesport Riesling
Harmonious, fruity and enjoyable with a country ham, and Chinese, Indian or Thai fare. $14.

1996 Jamesport Riesling
Lighter than its predecessor. Soft, aromatic, with traces of orange and green apple. $12.

1995 Jamesport Riesling
Lighthearted, but you may detect a lack of ripeness. Some peach and green apple notes. A sipper, chilled. $14.

1998 Laurel Lake Riesling
Floral and soft. Not much to it.
$10.

1997 Laurel Lake Riesling
For a riesling, lean. $13.

1999 Martha Clara Riesling
Balanced, floral and immediately likable, with fine fruit.
The pale yellow wine is decidedly dry. $15.

1999 Osprey's Dominion Johannisberg Riesling
Semi-dry, with lemony notes
and other citrus throughout. A
refresher to sample with shellfish. $13.

1998 Osprey's Dominion Johannisberg Riesling
Dry, peachy, floral, refreshing
and easy to drink. Citrusy finish. $13.

1997 Osprey's Dominion Johannisberg Riesling
Fruit and spice to spare in this
riesling, which seems like an
Alsatian snapshot compared
with earlier ones. $13.

1995 Osprey's Dominion Johannisberg Riesling
Peach and apricot in this
creamy wine, which is on the
sweet side. Serve chilled. $10.

1998 Palmer White Riesling
Vinified on the dry side, and
fine with crab cakes or a chicken pot pie. A pleasant and
uncomplicated wine for sipping, too. $14.

1997 Palmer White Riesling
Old sipper. $11.

2000 Paumanok Dry Riesling
A refreshing way to meet the
millennium. Young and vigorous, with notes of green apple.
Crisp and lively. Very good. $15.

**2000 Paumanok
Semi-Dry Riesling**
Appley, too. But there's more
peach-apricot here, and the
wine is more floral than its dry
friend. Sip solo or pair it with
oriental fare. $15.

**1999 Paumanok
Semi-Dry Riesling**
More dry than semi. Good, satisfying and right with spicier
dishes. $15.

1998 Paumanok Dry Riesling
Floral, youthful, attractive at
its release, the wine also has
improved over the last year or
so. Very Alsatian. $14.

**1998 Paumanok
Semi-Dry Riesling**
More floral than the dry, with
suggestions of peach. Instantly
likable. And a companion for
ham and loin of pork. $14.

**1997 Paumanok
Semi-Dry Riesling**
Delightful at the time. Hard to
find now. $14.

1995 Paumanok Riesling
A "semi-sweet table wine," with appealing tangelo flavors when released. Long gone. $10.

1998 Peconic Bay White Riesling
Good acidity and notes of grapefruit and pineapple are features of this tasty, aromatic wine. $12.

1996 Peconic Bay White Riesling
Hints of apple, some refreshing acidity. $11.

1995 Peconic Bay White Riesling
Pretty sweet, kind of old. $11

1996 Pindar Johannisberg Riesling
Sweetish, with traces of peach and melon. $9.

1999 Pugliese Riesling
Melon and orange notes in a light, unassuming refresher that goes with spicy foods or a ham. $10.

Sauvignon Blanc

Almost as recognizable as gewürztraminer is the zesty sauvignon blanc, which is high in acid and typically herbaceous. The aroma is pronounced. It's not a neutral wine.

Sauvignon blanc, or blanc fumé, shows off with flair in the Loire, with Sancerre and Pouilly-Fumé, California and New Zealand. The grape got a huge boost in the United States when Robert Mondavi created Fumé Blanc and heavily marketed the dry, oaky sauvignon blanc. It trails only chardonnay in California. Dry wines made from sauvignon blanc tend to be crisp. But the grape also leads to superb dessert wines. Sauvignon blanc contributes about one-fifth of the blend for the pinnacle of Sauternes, Chateau d'Yquem.

1996 Bidwell Sauvignon Blanc
Barrel-fermented, with hints of tropical fruit. Some citrus, too. Flinty and lean. Very good acidity. Right with spicy foods. $17.

1995 Bidwell Sauvignon Blanc
Fine varietal character: a little grassy, citrusy and herbal. Balanced and right, but at the end of the line. $18.

1999 Channing Perrine Sauvignon Blanc
Flinty, zesty, with lots of citrus and grassy notes. Made from North Fork grapes. $16.

1998 Channing Perrine Sauvignon Blanc
Snappy, herbaceous, summery wine. Also made from North Fork grapes. $16.

**1999 Hargrave
Sauvignon Blanc Reserve**
Peach and apricot notes are the surprises in this fine sauvignon blanc, which has a suggestion of oak, too. $15.

**1999 Hargrave
Sauvignon Blanc Reserve**
Herbaceous and floral, with a delicate aroma and good mouth-feel. A call to shellfish. $11.

1998 Hargrave Blanc Fumé
Lemony and still a little lively. $11.

1995 Hargrave Blanc Fumé
Pale yellow, with suggestions of honeysuckle. Fine acidity and no smokiness to distract you. Fruitier than the '94. $11.

**1998 Jamesport
Sauvignon Blanc**
Good varietal character, with citrus notes. Buttery, herbaceous. The winery's most spirited varietal. More versatile than the '97. $13

**1997 Jamesport
Sauvignon Blanc**
A racy, New Zealand relative. It was 70 percent barrel-fermented and also underwent a partial malolactic fermentation to tame some of the acidity. Light, lemony. $12

**1996 Jamesport
Sauvignon Blanc**
Light, green, lemony. $11

**1999 Macari
Sauvignon Blanc**
Very clean and crisp, with overtones of citrus and melon. Refreshing. $15

**1998 Osprey's Dominion
Sauvignon Blanc**
Plenty of citrus and some peach in this bright wine that's also slightly herbaceous. $12

**1998 Palmer
Sauvignon Blanc**
It doesn't overdo the herbaceous, green characteristics. More fruity and delicate, with some lemongrass zing. But drink it soon. $15

**1995 Palmer
Sauvignon Blanc**
The green grass and pungency of a Sancerre, if not the complexity, are in this late-inning refresher. $9

Semillon

Semillon makes wonderful wine when the grape rots nobly. It's often blended with sauvignon blanc, and hits stardom in Sauternes and Barsac, where golden dessert wines are made. This is the primary grape of Chateau d'Yquem. The dry whites of Graves highlight the union with sauvignon blanc, too.

The grape is planted in South Africa, New Zealand, Australia and the United States as well as France. Semillons have been produced successfully in the Pacific Northwest. On Long Island, there's minimal planting and, so far, one varietal.

1999 Martha Clara Semillon
The character of orange peel rises from this fruity, very accessible wine that has a golden hue. The aroma is appley. You'll like it with lightly sauced seafood. $15

Viognier

Viognier, the perfumed grape of the Rhône Valley, is at its best in Condrieu, the lovely French white.

Sometimes, it becomes a truly unusual partner: a rare appearance in Côte-Rôtie reds. Viognier is blended in the Languedoc-Roussillon region in the south, too.

The low-yield grape does make appearances in California, and in the mid-to-late 1990s started displaying its floral, apricot-peach qualities on Long Island. Expect to see more viognier, as an alternative to the major white varietals.

1999 Bedell Viognier
A delicate, rosy bouquet and melon notes define this lush, pleasurable, easy to like wine. $18

1998 Macari Viognier
Medium-bodied, floral charmer, low on acid and high in appeal. But it's close to passing its peak now. $14

1998 Bedell Viognier
Charming, dry and floral. Fruit-driven, with hints of honeysuckle. A youthful wine meant to be drunk last week. $18

1999 Martha Clara Viognier
Apricot, pear and melon thread their way through the crisp and very refreshing wine that's boosted with 12 percent chardonnay. Chinese and Thai fare are its partners. $15

1998 Pindar Viognier
Politely floral. Leaner than
before, but with a trace of
honey and spice. Light, diverting. $23

1996 Pindar Viognier
Lightly spicy, with a hint of
apricot. $19

1995 Pindar Viognier
This was the first of Long
Island's viogniers, and it was a
bright debut. Traces of pear.
It's going now. But worth a look
to see how the trendlet began.
$19

White Blends

The white combos, with a few exceptions, tend to be
sippers best consumed chilled and early.

Bedell Cygnet
Riesling, gewürztraminer and
summer days, when you want
something that's off-dry but
not off-putting. Picnics and
hors d'oeuvres. $8

**Bedell Cellars
Main Road White**
Chardonnay is added to the
blend for this one. Light and
fruity, with a dry finish. More
picnics. $8

**Duck Walk
Southampton White**
While on the subject of picnics.
A dry wine, part pinot gris,
part chardonnay. $9

Duck Walk Windmill White
Off-dry, routine. $8

Gristina Avalon
Sweet, forgettable, mostly riesling, upstate variety. $8

Hargrave Dune Blanc
Pinot blanc meets chardonnay.
Old now. $6

**Laurel Lake
Wind Song White**
The tune is sweet and very simple. $8

**1998 Palmer
Select Reserve White**
Well-crafted, spring-summer
union of chardonnay, sauvignon blanc, pinot blanc,
gewürztraminer. Generous with
fruit, green apple and lemon-lime. $17

**1997 Palmer
Select Reserve White**
A fine blend as above. The 15
percent of gewürztraminer is
the curve, providing a very
fruity finish. $15

Paumanok Festival White
Light, on the sweet side. $8

**1997 Peconic Bay
Vin de l'Ile Blanc**
Past its modest prime. $11

**1998 Pellegrini East End
Commonage White**
Tasting-room decoration. $7

Pindar Autumn Gold
Wine lite, with an upstate
accent. $8

Pindar Winter White
Mild thing. $8

**1999 Schneider
Potato Barn White**
The latest version of the
chardonnay with a splash of
pinot blanc, steel-fermented.
Clean, with notes of apricot
and peach. $13

**1998 Schneider
Potato Barn White**
Chardonnay with a shot of
pinot blanc add up to a balanced, light wine, with a hint of
pear. $13

Ripening merlot

Chapter 4

The Palette
of Reds

Merlot madness, cabernet rising

Long Island is New York State's haven for the classic red grape varieties, such as merlot and cabernet sauvignon.

Red wines come in many shades, from the purplish tint of youth to the brick red of maturity. The grapes themselves are reddish and often closer to blue. Some look black. A red wine gets its color when the juice of the grapes contacts the skins during fermentation. The skins also impart tannins, the compounds that give wine astringency and act as a preservative, lengthening a wine's life.

In addition to cabernet sauvignon and merlot, red wine grapes include cabernet franc, gamay, grenache, nebbiolo, pinot noir, sangiovese, syrah and zinfandel.

Following are descriptions of the red wine grapes of Long Island, and reviews of selected Long Island wines made from them. Red blends are included.

Cabernet Franc

This grape long has been known as a blending companion for cabernet sauvignon, the greatest of red wine grapes.

Cabernet franc is a popular, cool-weather planting in Bordeaux, especially in the districts of Pomerol and Saint-Émilion; the Loire Valley; southwest France; and Friuli-Venezia Giulia in northern Italy. It's a plumper, juicier and less tannic grape than cabernet sauvignon and is defined by soft, fruity flavors.

The summit of cabernet franc is attained by Chateau Cheval Blanc in Saint-Émilion. At considerably less cost, you could try the wines from Bergerac, Bourgueil, Chinon and Madiran.

More of the varietal is being planted on Long Island, and many of the initial wines have been very good. The climate and the soil point to a sound future. The early-maturing grape could be the next big red here. Schneider Vineyards in particular proclaims cabernet franc as its primary grape.

1997 Bidwell Barrel Sample Cabernet Franc
Chewy for a cabernet franc. Good fruit and concentrated flavor. Available only at the winery. $35.

1994 Bidwell Cabernet Franc
Cherry and raspberry notes. Bright color, good flavor. $23.

1998 Corey Creek Cabernet Franc
Full of blackberry and raspberry, and smoky nuances from the oak. Smooth, with a bit of cabernet sauvignon added. $19.

1997 Corey Creek Cabernet Franc
Generous fruitiness. Round, bright, toasty. Very smooth. $18.

1997 Gristina Cabernet Franc
Intensely fruity, with loads of black cherry and blackberry nuances. A smooth, attractive cabernet franc with real structure and depth. $20.

**1998 Hargrave
Cabernet Franc Reserve**
Vibrant and gutsy, the wine has fine varietal character and power, too. Serious cabernet franc, with a longer life than most. $22.

**1998 Hargrave
Cabernet Franc**
Lots of spice and blackberries in this cabernet franc. Traces of pepperiness, too. Pairs well with rustic dishes. $17.

**1997 Hargrave
Cabernet Franc**
One of the better cabernet francs from this vineyard, with firmness and finesse. Good fruit. $14.

**1995 Hargrave
Cabernet Franc**
Proof that this grape isn't just for blending. Lots of dark fruit and spiciness. But relaxed. $14.

**1994 Hargrave
Cabernet Franc**
Tight and tannic. $13.

**1993 Hargrave
Cabernet Franc**
Loads of fruit, mainly cherry, in this full-bodied, slightly earthy cabernet that's at its height now. $14.

**1997 Jamesport
Cabernet Franc**
Full of berry flavors. A fairly light, accessible red. $18.

**1995 Jamesport
Cabernet Franc**
Cedar and cherry notes are in this ruby-shaded wine. Traces of spice and mint. But on the lean side. $15.

1997 Macari Cabernet Franc
Spiciness and nuances of cherry, cedar and ripe fruit. A supple and smooth cabernet to drink now. $19.

**1998 Osprey's Dominion
Cabernet Franc**
The winery's first. It has a suggestion of candied fruit, mainly raspberry and cherry. Good body, versatile. $15.

1998 Palmer Cabernet Franc
Soft tannins, cherry and currant notes, lighter style than '97. $18.

1997 Palmer Cabernet Franc
Fruit-driven, with good structure and cherry accents. $17.

1995 Palmer Cabernet Franc
Full, ripe, soft, with traces of dried cherry. $15.

1994 Palmer Cabernet Franc
Fruitier, fuller, earthier than the '93, with blueberry notes still there. $15.

1993 Palmer Cabernet Franc
Spirited red that has some time left. Less herbaceous than usual. High acidity. Made with 14 percent merlot and 11 per-

cent cabernet sauvignon. $14.

**1998 Paumanok
Cabernet Franc**
Pretty light, more summery
than wintry. But it has very
good varietal character and up-
front fruit. $18.

**1998 Peconic Bay
Cabernet Franc**
Balanced, with good black fruit,
some oak and a suggestion of
pepperiness. Very good. $20.

**1997 Peconic Bay
Cabernet Franc**
Modest and a bit lean. $10.

**1998 Pellegrini
Cabernet Franc**
Herbaceous, rife with berry
qualities. Smooth. $17.

**1997 Pellegrini
Cabernet Franc**
Big, juicy varietal, with berry
notes and some spiciness.
Notably long finish. $17.

**1996 Pellegrini
Cabernet Franc**
Medium-bodied, with aspects of
blueberry and spice. Not up to
the '95 and '97. $17.

**1995 Pellegrini
Cabernet Franc**
Concentrated, ripe. Notes of
mint and raspberry. A bigger
version of the '94. $23.

1994 Pindar Cabernet Franc
Soft and approachable. Very
up-front. $19.

**1998 Pugliese
Cabernet Franc**
Easygoing, with a touch of oak-
iness. Black cherry notes. $15.

**1998 Schneider
Cabernet Franc**
Ripe, inky, heady with dried
fruit aromas and a whiff of
anise. Traces of vanilla. Very
smooth, with enough structure
to last several years. Made at
Bedell Cellars. $24.

**1997 Schneider
Cabernet Franc**
Elegant and juicy, with some
merlot and cabernet sauvignon
to finish it. Full and balanced.
Barrel-aged 14 months. Made
at Bedell, with Macari grapes.
$23.

**1995 Schneider
Cabernet Franc**
Better than the auspicious '94.
Bright, fruity, elegant, with con-
siderable character and struc-
ture. $21.

**1994 Schneider
Cabernet Franc**
Delightful debut for the vint-
ners. Harmony and spice. $19.

Cabernet Sauvignon

The essence of Bordeaux, cabernet sauvignon yields those slowly maturing, complex wines of legend, among them Chateaux Latour, Lafite-Rothschild and Mouton-Rothschild.

California's noblest reds are cabernet sauvignon, too, from producers such as Beaulieu, Caymus, Chateau Montelena, Heitz, Jordan, Joseph Phelps, Robert Mondavi and Stag's Leap Wine Cellars. The grape is important in Italy's "super-Tuscans," such as Ornellaia, Sassicaia, Solaia and Tignanello.

Cabernet sauvignon also is planted extensively in Australia, Chile and parts of eastern Europe. Its profile is rising in Spain, where cabernet sauvignon is blended with tempranillo.

The small, blue-black, thick-skinned, low-yielding, meaty grape ripens late and prospers in austere soil. What it needs is good drainage. And, after the wine is made, time.

Cabernet sauvignon wines at first may seem very tight and unyielding, tannic and astringent. The structure and depth of the wine depends on the initially unfriendly strong tannins and acids. They do, however, give the finest cabernets such long, elegant lives.

A long growing season and warm weather are essential. On Long Island, cabernet sauvignon does well only in years when the hot, dry weather persists. The '90s have been uncommonly generous, so much so that several of the region's highly recommended wines are from this king of grapes.

1997 Bedell
Cabernet Sauvignon
Excellent fruit. Hints of cassis, cherry, chocolate and spice. Supple and showing depth, the wine has considerable finesse. A refined, elegant cabernet with time to spare. Not as big as the '95, but easily recommended in its own way. $25.

1995 Bedell
Cabernet Sauvignon
Big, rich, terrific. Lots of black fruit, a hint of chocolate, blueberry notes. The wine has plenty of spine and has developed well since release. It should do so for years ahead. Deserves more time. $22.

1994 Bedell
Cabernet Sauvignon
The tannins have softened. The fruit is ripe in this opulent, harmonious production that leads to a long, lovely finish. Cassis, clove and hints of mint. $20.

**1993 Bedell
Cabernet Sauvignon**
Plenty of muscle in this vibrant wine, along with ample black fruit and sweet oak. Cassis and vanilla run through it. Long finish. $16.

**1996 Bidwell
Cabernet Sauvignon**
Full-bodied, minerally and tannic. The wine remains a little tight. $20.

**1994 Bidwell
Cabernet Sauvignon**
A re-release of the cabernet. Announcing itself with balance, good fruit, soft tannins, finesse. $35.

**1997 Duck Walk Cabernet
Sauvignon Reserve**
Full and hearty, with suggestions of black cherry and plum. Firm structure, long finish, maturing well. On sale at the winery. $25.

**1997 Duck Walk
Cabernet Sauvignon**
In some ways, more appealing than the reserve. Round, displaying cassis and blackberry notes. $15.

**1995 Duck Walk
Cabernet Sauvignon**
Versatile, husky, full-bodied, with some cherry notes. Not very smooth. $19.

**1994 Duck Walk
Cabernet Sauvignon**
Black cherry nuances in a blunt red. Long finish. Not a study in finesse. $19.

**1998 Gristina
Cabernet Sauvignon**
A light cabernet for this winery, with up-front fruit. Medium-bodied. Traces of mint, plum, chocolate. $20.

**1997 Gristina
Cabernet Sauvignon**
Big, with deep color and considerable complexity. Chocolate notes, some plum, much cassis. $18.

**1996 Gristina
Cabernet Sauvignon**
Not on a par with the '95. Agreeable but not long-lived. $16.

**1995 Gristina Andy's Field
Cabernet Sauvignon**
Concentrated cabernet that's elegant and refined, with much flavor and a lot of black fruit. It's tannic and needs more time. Expect it to develop well into the decade. $28.

**1995 Gristina
Cabernet Sauvignon**
Concentrated, supple red with merlot properties and traces of black cherry. $16.

**1993 Gristina
Cabernet Sauvignon**
Depth and body, very concen-

trated, with hints of cedar and currant. $16.

1992 Gristina
Cabernet Sauvignon

Tannic at the outset, it has mellowed. Traces of currant and coffee. $14.

1998 Hargrave Cabernet
Sauvignon Reserve

Very much a Bordeaux taking the local. Fine fruit, structure, depth, with hints of chocolate. Expertly done. Should last several years. $32.

1993 Hargrave QED
Cabernet Sauvignon

As in "quod erat demonstrandum." And, as the phrase suggests, it has been shown that outstanding cabernet sauvignon can be made on the North Fork. Now, this is a Castello di Borghese-Hargrave library selection. Big, deep, with remarkable complexity. Some briariness from cabernet franc, the blueberry of a ripe merlot and the cassis, leathery contribution of cabernet sauvignon. Symphonic wine. $40.

1998 Laurel Lake Cabernet
Sauvignon Reserve

Ruby-shaded, tannins to spare. Good fruit, balance, hints of smoothness to come. $18.

1998 Laurel Lake
Cabernet Sauvignon

The little brother, smoky, tannic and tight. $15.

1995 Laurel Lake
Cabernet Sauvignon

It has gotten better, opening up to show good fruit. $18.

1997 Lenz Estate
Cabernet Sauvignon

Big and impressive, with excellent fruit, softening tannins, considerable structure. It could pass for a ripe Bordeaux. $30.

1995 Lenz Estate
Cabernet Sauvignon

Big, extracted wine that continues to age gracefully. Fine-tuned with merlot. The first impression was Napa Valley. Now, Bordeaux. $28.

1994 Lenz Estate
Cabernet Sauvignon

Balanced, opening up. Minerally, still tannic. But there are years left for it to mature. $25.

1993 Lenz Vineyard Selection
Cabernet Sauvignon

Raspberry and red fruit, soft tannins, some earthiness, a touch of sweetness. Seems almost Californian. $15.

1998 Loughlin
Cabernet Sauvignon

Closed and pretty tannic right now. An undercurrent of good fruit. Should get better. Made at Peconic Bay Winery. $20.

1996 Loughlin
Cabernet Sauvignon

Tight, short on ripeness. $17.

1997 Osprey's Dominion Cabernet Sauvignon
Chocolate, cedar notes, a suggestion of blackberry. $15.

1995 Osprey's Dominion Reserve Cabernet Sauvignon
Big and bold, with firm structure, fine fruit and aging potential. $25.

1995 Osprey's Dominion Cabernet Sauvignon
Full-bodied, with traces of chocolate, licorice, some black pepper, toasty oak. $15.

1993 Osprey's Dominion Cabernet Sauvignon
Oakier and fruitier than the '95 and not as intense. Some cherry notes. $15.

1998 Palmer Cabernet Sauvignon
Softer style, more red fruit than black, with some earthy notes. $14.

1997 Palmer Reserve Cabernet Sauvignon
Palmer's first reserve cabernet. Tannic initially, but opens up to display intensity of the fruit, undertones of chocolate and coffee. Merlot and cabernet franc were added to soften it. Young. Give it time. $18.

1995 Palmer Cabernet Sauvignon
Very smooth and mature. Good berry fruit, big tannic structure.
Also has a shot of merlot and a bit of cabernet franc. $13.

1994 Palmer Cabernet Sauvignon
Medium-bodied, with cherry notes. Smooth tannins. Passing its prime. $13.

1998 Paumanok Cabernet Sauvignon
Much fruitiness and good structure here. And immediately drinkable. Soft tannins. $18.

1997 Paumanok Cabernet Sauvignon
Smooth, soft wine with some finesse that's ready to drink. Not as big as the memorable '95 or the '93, but recommended on its own. Black fruit, cherry notes. $17.

1995 Paumanok Limited Edition Tuthills Lane Cabernet Sauvignon
A stunner that should have a long stay in cellars. There probably aren't that many bottles left. Worth the search. Great fruit is only the start. Firm tannins, concentrated flavors, grand mouth-feel. It has depth and style, elegance and power. A Sugar Ray of a wine. $40.

1995 Paumanok Grand Vintage Cabernet Sauvignon
Excellent cabernet and a fabulous alternative to the Limited Edition Tuthills Lane. Full of fruit and mint, fine mouth-feel.

Age-worthy, delightful. $22.

**1994 Paumanok
Cabernet Sauvignon**
Lighter, with notes of black currant and cherry. Drink now. $13.

**1993 Paumanok Grand
Vintage Cabernet Sauvignon**
Supple and as easy to recommend as it is difficult to locate.
Blackberry, plum, toasty oak, ripeness, long finish. $22.

**1998 Peconic Bay
Cabernet Sauvignon**
Tannic, with too much bite. $17.

**1994 Peconic Bay
Cabernet Sauvignon**
Blunt red. Slight note of blackberry. $20.

**1998 Pellegrini
Cabernet Sauvignon**
Very good fruit. The tannins are there and need to soften. A wine with potential to grow. $17.

**1997 Pellegrini
Cabernet Sauvignon**
Cedary, with lots of black fruit and a suggestion of chocolate.
It should soften and unfold over the next two or three years. $17.

**1996 Pellegrini
Cabernet Sauvignon**
More closed than not. $16.

**1995 Pellegrini
Cabernet Sauvignon**
Deep and ripe, with firm tannins, cassis and dark fruit. It has evolved very well since release and could use more time. Excellent structure, wonderful wine. $15.

**1994 Pellegrini
Cabernet Sauvignon**
Balanced, full-bodied, slightly tannic, hints of plum. $15.

**1993 Pellegrini
Cabernet Sauvignon**
Dark and intense, with generous fruit. Traces of cassis and mint, with enough oak and tannin, too. Approaching its peak.
Worth seeking. $15.

**1995 Pindar Reserve
Cabernet Sauvignon**
Age-worthy and big.
Undercurrents of bell pepper, ripe black fruit, raspberry.
Ready for a ribeye steak. Or wait five years and make it a porterhouse. $18.

**1994 Pindar
Cabernet Sauvignon**
Blunt and tannic. $19.

**1993 Pindar Reserve
Cabernet Sauvignon**
Concentrated, heavy-duty dry wine, with aspects of cherry.
$17.

**1997 Pugliese Cabernet
Sauvignon Reserve**
Meaty, chewy red, with good fruit. $14.

1996 Pugliese
Cabernet Sauvignon
Tight and tannic. $14.

1995 Pugliese
Cabernet Sauvignon
No-nonsense red to go with a
wintry meal. $14.

1994 Pugliese
Cabernet Sauvignon
Much the same as the '95. $14.

1993 Pugliese
Cabernet Sauvignon
Straightforward, medium-bod-
ied. $14.

1997 Ternhaven
Cabernet Sauvignon
Black cherry notes, good
mouth-feel. Try it with a ripe
Stilton. $21.

1996 Ternhaven
Cabernet Sauvignon
Softened since release, but still
tight. $12.

1995 Ternhaven
Cabernet Sauvignon
Big and full, with fairly soft
tannins and cassis notes. $20.

1994 Ternhaven
Cabernet Sauvignon
Rough-hewn early effort. $16.

Gamay

Gamay is the prince of Beaujolais. It's a grape low in
tannin, high in acid.

The wines are very fruity, very friendly and more purple
than Barney.

Sometimes, gamay is blended with other varieties. Much
of the gamay in the United States may not be connected to
the true grape, but is more likely a clone of pinot noir.
Anyway, they're all fruity and meant to be drunk young.

2000 Osprey's Dominion
Gamay Noir
Fruity and friendly, versatile
and to be consumed immediately with casual fare, or pretty
much whatever you're eating
now. $18.

1998 Pindar Gamay Beaujolais
That label dances off the shelf
and so does the light, unpretentious, grapey wine it advertises.
Picnics year-round. $9.

1996 Pindar Gamay Beaujolais
Bright in its youth. Past prime.
$9.

Merlot

Merlot has reined in white-wine drinkers and attracted many others to reds. It's much softer, less tannic and less demanding than cabernet sauvignon and ripens earlier, yielding rounder wines. Merlots also develop faster than cabernet sauvignon.

In Bordeaux, it has been the primary blending grape for cabernet sauvignon and it's the most planted. But in the cooler regions of Bordeaux, Pomerol and Saint-Émilion, the thin-skinned, dark blue merlot is the main grape. The great Chateau Petrus is made with merlot.

This grape is a dependable varietal in the Veneto in Italy, Argentina, California and Washington State. From California, in particular, look for the merlots of Duckhorn, Leonetti, Newton and Niebaum-Coppola.

So far, it's handily the East End's most planted and most sought red.

1997 Bedell Merlot Reserve
Big and beautiful, with years ahead. The wine at first is tight and unwilling to unveil itself. But give it time. The structure is firm, and the notes of berry and plum are starting to show. One of the best. $30.

1997 Bedell Merlot
Juicy and very fruity, with generous plum qualities and ripe berry notes. It has finesse. $18.

1996 Bedell Merlot
Better to try this one earlier instead of later. Fruity, easygoing, on the lighter side. $18.

1995 Bedell Merlot Reserve
A bright star of the vintage, concentrated, full-bodied and maturing well. Vivid black fruit and ample toasty oak, great color and a rich life ahead. Textbook. $28.

1995 Bedell Merlot
Fruity and balanced, supple, ripe and plummy. Cherry notes, too. Ready to drink. $18.

1994 Bedell Merlot Reserve
Berry-picking time. A soft and smooth merlot with fine fruit and finesse. $28.

1994 Bedell Merlot
Typically well-done and more Bordeaux in style. $16.

1993 Bedell Merlot Reserve
Exceptional. Vibrant black fruit, cherry and currant. Hints of vanilla. Opulent, with those tannins smoothing out. More Californian. $28.

1995 Bidwell
Merlot Barrel Sample
Lots of plumminess and a long finish. Balanced, jammy, fruity, with traces of spice. $30.

1993 Bidwell Merlot
Plummy and smoky, with a long finish. $23.

1994 Channing Daughters
Sculpture Garden Merlot
Dubbed a Library Selection, the wine could still use some time on the shelf. But it's fruity and toasty, with plum notes. $25.

1998 Corey Creek Merlot
Cherry notes highlight this satisfying, still slightly tannic red. Needs time to develop, and should do so nicely. $19.

1997 Corey Creek Merlot
Very fruity, lightly herbaceous, with traces of cherry. It has finesse. $18.

1996 Corey Creek Merlot
Medium-bodied, with nuances of black fruit. Good, considering the vintage. $18.

1995 Corey Creek Merlot
Dense and ripe. One of the best from the winery. $17.

1993 Corey Creek Merlot
Ripe, with a hint of berries. $16.

1997 Duck Walk Merlot
Some plum notes and to the point. $15.

1995 Duck Walk
Special Reserve Merlot
A limited-edition number, ripe and ambitious. Sold at the winery. Hard to find. If you do, enjoy. $27.

1995 Duck Walk
Merlot Reserve
Juicy and big, lots of plumminess and oak. Full-flavored fare goes with it. $19.

1994 Duck Walk
Merlot Reserve
Black fruit flavors, ripe and ready. $20.

1994 Duck Walk Merlot
Good fruit and varietal character. $17.

1998 Gristina Merlot
Berry notes. Balanced and developing. It's 15 percent cabernet sauvignon. $20.

1997 Gristina
Andy's Field Merlot
Ripe, dark, deeply plummy and continuing to mature. This one should last a while. Very good structure, first-rate fruit. $27.

1997 Gristina Merlot
Just showing its strengths. Fine fruit and structure. At first, seemed closed, but it has matured well. $17.

1995 Gristina
Andy's Field Merlot
Deep, complex and satisfying,

alive with black fruit. There's assertive oak. The wine has firm structure and is reaching its peak. $27.

1994 Gristina
Andy's Field Merlot

Juicy and ripe, with suggestions of plum and prune. $27.

1993 Gristina
Andy's Field Merlot

Among the outstanding merlots of the year. It has aged very well. A terrific wine. $27.

1993 Gristina Merlot

Black fruit and a suggestion of mint run through this wine. Passing its prime. $15.

1998 Hargrave
Merlot Reserve

Fruity, lightly tannic, with a fugitive floral aroma and finesse. Balanced. Ready to drink. $25.

1998 Hargrave Merlot

Traces of rose petal in this fruity, balanced merlot. $18.

1995 Hargrave
Lattice Label Merlot

For what initially seemed like a wine to age, this has turned into a surprisingly early drinker. Ample fruitiness, harmony; violet and vivid. Contains some cabernet sauvignon. $18.

1994 Hargrave Merlot

Soft, full of fruit, very accessible. $16.

1993 Hargrave
Lattice Label Merlot

First-class wine that wears that lattice label like a crown. Mature, refined, with suggestions of red fruit and herbs. Ready to drink. $27.

1997 Jamesport
Merlot Estate

Very good, plummy merlot, with a diverting chocolate note. $19.

1996 Jamesport
Merlot Estate

Lean. $14.

1995 Jamesport
Church Field Merlot

Fine, deep ruby production. Balanced, with berry and chocolate accents, plus a touch of anise. It's 17 percent cabernet sauvignon, 8 percent cabernet franc. $18.

1995 Jamesport Merlot

Clean, quite fruity, emphasis on cherry. Workmanlike, easygoing. $16.

1994 Jamesport Merlot

Soft and accessible varietal, but passing its prime. $16.

1993 Jamesport
Merlot Reserve

Ripe fruit, good varietal character. $20.

1998 Laurel Lake Merlot

Lean. $13.

1996 Laurel Lake Merlot
Forgettable. $13.

1998 Lenz Reserve Merlot
About as up-front as a Lenz
merlot gets, and a reminder of
the '97 merlot-cabernet sauvignon blend. Fruity and immediate. $17.

**1997 Lenz Estate
Bottled Merlot**
A big, gorgeous wine, perhaps
the best ever from this winery.
Concentrated, rich, maturing
slowly. Some cabernet sauvignon and cabernet franc are in
the production. The vines that
contributed are 19 years old.
One of the merlots that should
test how well this varietal ages
around here. $55.

**1997 Lenz Vineyard
Selection Merlot**
Very good fruit, very accessible
wine. From much younger vines
than the Estate Bottled star.
But satisfying, solid, easily recommended. $25.

**1996 Lenz Estate
Bottled Merlot**
Satisfactory only, from a trou-
bled vintage. $25.

**1996 Lenz Vineyard
Selection Merlot**
Light, tight, less fruity than
what came before and after.
$17.

**1995 Lenz Estate
Bottled Merlot**
Deep and delicious, round and
rich. A masterful marriage of
berry fruit and oak. Very
impressive when first tasted,
more so now. $40.

**Lenz Vineyard
Selection Merlot**
Non-vintage varietal from 1995
and '96. Balanced, concentrated, with ripe fruit and mellow
tannins. A winner. $15

**1994 Lenz Estate
Bottled Merlot**
Opulent, ripe with black fruit.
Lots of up-front pleasure, with
nuances of plum and berry. The
wine could mature some more.
$30.

**1993 Lenz Estate
Bottled Merlot**
Excellent wine. Reductive fla-
vors, plummy and berry-filled.
Ripe and drinking well. $25.

1998 Lieb Merlot
Plummy, up-front merlot with
very good varietal character.
It's the first merlot under the
Lieb label. Made at Paumanok
Vineyards. $19.

1999 Loughlin Merlot
Tight now. But should open up.
Tasted early. $22.

1998 Macari Merlot
Good fruit, with plum notes
and up-front appeal. $24.

1997 Macari Merlot
Subtle and satisfying, with plenty of plumminess and spice. Enough tannin for heft. Plump and well-knit. $22.

1996 Macari Merlot
Respectable, light first effort, with cedar notes. But tight. $16.

1998 Osprey's Dominion Merlot
Sweet notes of cherry and chocolate in this wine tailored for red meat. $18.

1997 Osprey's Dominion Merlot
Very fruity, red variety. Toasty notes. Flavorful and good. $16.

1995 Osprey's Dominion Merlot
Fruity, fairly light, with traces of plum. $15.

1993 Osprey's Dominion Merlot
Spicy, oaky, grapey, better with food than without. Made at Palmer Vineyards. $14.

1997 Palmer Reserve Merlot
Very big red, well-structured and impressive, and a candidate for Palmer's best merlot. The wine needs time. Tannins are softening. Have some patience. $30.

1997 Palmer Merlot
Fruity, not overly oaked. Good result. $18.

Palmer Merlot
A non-vintage wine from the slow-ripening '96 harvest, supplemented by lots from the '95. Rough-hewn. $14.

1996 Palmer Merlot
Tight wine from a lesser year. $18.

1995 Palmer Reserve Merlot
Jammy and ripe, lots of plum, prune and cherry character, with spicy undertones. Heavy oak. Long finish. $29.

1994 Palmer Merlot
Neat balance of sweet fruit and oak, round and attractive, with hints of raspberry. $15.

1998 Paumanok Merlot
Soft and very smooth, with good body and lively red fruit. Instantly accessible. $18.

1997 Paumanok Merlot
Smooth, clean, definitely for dinner tonight. Fine fruit, generous varietal character. $18.

1996 Paumanok Merlot
Berry notes, a little tannic, not too complicated. $14.

1995 Paumanok Grand Vintage Merlot
It has evolved into a marvelous wine, heady with varietal character. Velvety finish. Here for the long haul. $22.

1993 Paumanok Grand Vintage Merlot
Softer, fruitier and very good. Also with considerable life. Neatly balanced. Blackberry and spice. $19.

1997 Peconic Bay Epic Acre Merlot
Not as epic as the '95. But the fruit is good and the finish is long. $25.

1995 Peconic Bay Epic Acre Merlot
Full-bodied, with excellent black fruit, plenty of spine and a vibrant ruby shade en route to black. $25.

1995 Peconic Bay Merlot
Blackberry, peppery notes. But tannic. $20.

1994 Peconic Bay Merlot
Fruitier, full-bodied, with 15 percent cabernet sauvignon. $20.

1998 Pellegrini Merlot
Fruity and satisfying with good varietal character. Tasted early. Could use a little time. $17.

1997 Pellegrini Merlot
Much fine fruit, suggestions of chocolate and coffee. Very good. $17.

1996 Pellegrini Merlot
Cherry and plum notes in this medium-bodied, satisfactory red. $17.

1995 Pellegrini Merlot
Cassis and blackberry flavors, in a merlot with excellent fruit and touches of oak. Very good. $17.

1994 Pellegrini Merlot
Plummy, with blueberry notes. Aromatic and very fruity. Low tannin. Drink it now. $27.

1993 Pellegrini Merlot
A big, tannic merlot, with its elegance unfolded. Generous ripeness. $17.

1998 Pindar Reserve Merlot
Satisfactory varietal character, but needs to open up a bit. $19.

1997 Pindar Merlot
Good, fruity, with black cherry and plum notes. $15.

1995 Pindar Merlot
Neatly styled. Very good fruit, mainly cherry. An oak lining. $19.

1994 Pindar Reserve Merlot
Fruity, accessible, but getting old. $19.

1993 Pindar Reserve Merlot
Much better than when released. Oaky, plummy, full-bodied. $15.

1997 Pugliese Merlot Reserve
Long finish, supple wine with hints of plum. $14.

1996 Pugliese Merlot
Uncomplicated, with a cherry
note. $14.

1995 Pugliese Merlot
Lean. $14.

1994 Pugliese Merlot Reserve
Flavorful, with traces of cherry.
$14.

1993 Pugliese Merlot Reserve
More fruity than tannic, with
hints of sweetness. $14.

1997 Raphael Merlot
The first wine from Raphael,
and it shows great promise.
Layers of good fruit and distinct varietal character. Finesse
and complexity. Tasted early.
$35.

1998 Schneider Merlot
Berry-rich, plummy merlot,
round and big. It can age a bit.
$23.

1997 Schneider Merlot
Lively, with plum and cassis.
Smooth and attractive, with 20
percent cabernet franc. Made
with Macari grapes at Bedell.
$23.

1994 Schneider Merlot
Dry, balanced, attractive. Also
via Macari and Bedell. $19.

1997 Ternhaven Merlot
Much better than the '96, with
sweet fruit and a hint of spice.
$22.

1996 Ternhaven Merlot
Some fruit notes, but lean. $18.

1995 Ternhaven Merlot
Up-front berry fruit. Dry.
Improves on the '94. $18.

**1998 Wölffer Estate
Selection Merlot**
Ripe, plummy, with good varietal character. Not the '97, but
a commendable wine with firm
structure. $29.

**1998 Wölffer La Ferme
Martin Merlot**
Lively, full of berry flavors.
Medium-bodied. Fire up the
barbecue. $14.

**1997 Wölffer Estate
Selection Merlot**
Concentrated and complex, it's
Wölffer at its best. Great fruit,
soft tannins, ample structure.
A superb wine, alive with the
aroma of black currants and
ripe plums. Long finish. The
wine will last several years
before accompanying beef or
lamb. $30.

1997 Wölffer Merlot
A very sophisticated younger
relative of the Estate Selection,
with ripe fruit and softer tannins. $19.

1996 Wölffer Merlot
Some cherry notes. But lean.
$18.

**1995 Wölffer Estate
Selection Merlot**
Full-bodied and opulent, generous with cherry and plum.
Spice notes. The wine has depth and finesse, and years to go. $30.

1995 Wölffer Merlot
Ripe fruit, hints of cassis and anise. Deep color. Oakiness on the finish. $19.

1994 Wölffer Merlot
Hard early and past prime. $14.

Pinot Meunier

Pinot meunier finds its fame in Champagne. Along with the dominant pinot noir and chardonnay, pinot meunier often is in the blend. The cool-weather grape is fruitier than its companions. To find a still wine made with pinot meunier, you'll have to look toward Australia and Germany. Or at least to Peconic and Water Mill.

**1997 Duck Walk
Pinot Meunier**
The lone ranger of this varietal around here. Fruity, with traces of plum. Worth trying. $13.

**1995 Duck Walk
Pinot Meunier**
Traces of plum and black currant highlight this pinot. It has flair. $13.

Pinot Noir

The temperamental and finicky, seductive grape of Burgundy also makes the base wine for Champagne.

Pinot noir buds early and doesn't yield a lot. More than with many other grapes, you need good fortune as well as good climate and soil. Not as tannic as cabernet sauvignon, it produces wines of many styles.

The height of pinot noir, in price and quality, is reached astronomically with the wines of the Romanée-Conti estate. Among Burgundy's fine producers of red wine are Domaine Comte de Vogue, Domaine Leroy and Domaine Henri Jayer. The names on many of the wines read like a vinous all-star team: Aloxe-Corton, Chambertin, Clos de Vougeot, Echezeaux, Musigny, Nuits-St-Georges, Pommard, Richebourg, La Tâche, Volnay, Vosne-Romanée and Romanée-Conti itself.

Pinot noir's advocates in the Pacific Northwest include Adelsheim, Calera, Domaine Drouhin and Ponzi. In California, Au Bon Climat and J. Rochioli make notable pinots. The grape has had some success on Long Island, in a few cases yielding exceptional wines.

1998 Gristina Pinot Noir
An earthy, soulful pinot, with traces of cola, spice and vanilla. Floral, fragrant. It has heft. $30.

1994 Gristina Pinot Noir
Inviting, with a hint of violet as a lagniappe. $25.

1993 Gristina Pinot Noir
Woodsy, earthy, with a hint of mushrooms, cherries and blackberries. $25.

1998 Hargrave Pinot Noir
Under the Castello di Borghese-Hargrave label. Earthy and aromatic, very smooth, with a map of Burgundy as its template. $32.

1997 Hargrave Pinot Noir
Not the big-time "Le Noirien," but smooth and harmonious. Soft tannins, very good fruit. $17.

**1995 Hargrave
Pinot Noir "Le Noirien"**
Silky, elegant and superb. The name stems from the old title for pinot noir in Burgundy. Supple, with hints of black cherry and spice. One of the family jewels. $35.

**1993 Hargrave
Pinot Noir "Le Noirien"**
Rich, opulent, fabulous drink-ing. Among the best of the locals. Check the archives. $35.

1998 Jamesport Pinot Noir
Cola, cranberry notes and smoky nuances are in this straightforward, earthy pinot. Moderate tannins. $18.

1995 Lenz Pinot Noir
Concentrated and rich. Fullness in mouth-feel. Softer, not as reductive as the '93; suggests the Pacific Northwest more than Burgundy. $15.

1993 Lenz Pinot Noir
Mushrooms abound in this forest of a wine, which hints at dried fruit and the good earth. $25.

**1998 Osprey's Dominion
Pinot Noir**
Tannins have settled down. Lively spice and fruit. Some vanilla. $22.

**1997 Osprey's Dominion
Pinot Noir**
Satisfying, straightforward. A wine for autumn nights. $22.

**1996 Osprey's Dominion
Pinot Noir**
Medium-bodied, light on tannin, currant notes. Satisfactory. $16.

1995 Wölffer Pinot Noir
An elegant, remarkable full-bodied red made from grapes grown in Manorville. The color is deep and so's the flavor. Dried cherry and plum accents. Chestnuts, too. $35.

Sangiovese

Sangiovese is the primary grape in Chianti, and widely planted in Tuscany and southern Italy. Sometimes, cabernet sauvignon is blended with sangiovese, giving the wine more spine and a longer life.

A strain of sangiovese called brunello is the grape of the classic Brunello di Montalcino. Altesino, Barbi, Biondi-Santi, Banfi, Lisini and Pertimali are among the notable producers. For sangiovese-based wines, such as the Chiantis, look once more for Altesino, as well as Antinori, Badia a Coltibuono, Monsanto, Nozzole and Ruffino.

Sangiovese also is doing well, but on a very limited scale, in California. Atlas Peak, Beaulieu, Ferrari-Carano and Luna are commendable labels.

Although few wines have been made so far, it's a grape with a future on Long Island.

1999 Pugliese Sangiovese
Medium-bodied and flavorful, with up-front fruit, earthiness and tame tannin. Versatile and likable from the first sip. Pugliese planted one-half acre of sangiovese more than a decade ago, after lightning struck some of the merlot vines. A bolt of inspiration. $15.

1998 Pugliese Sangiovese
The local Chianti. Light, fruity, flavorful wine, and a friend to many dishes. Dry, with a hint of cherry. Very drinkable. $15.

Syrah

The classic red grape of the Rhône region is the source of tannic, deep, long-lived wines. From the northern Rhône come Cornas, Côte-Rotie, Crozes-Hermitage and Hermitage. Châteauneuf-du-Pape in the southern Rhône and Provence also have syrah plantings.

In Australia, syrah is shiraz, and it contributes to wines ranging from modest to grand. The greatest is Grange, from Penfolds. In the United States, Dehlinger and Swanson have made impressive syrah-based wines. The grape is only beginning to take hold on Long Island.

1997 Pindar Syrah
Potent and brawny, it's a muscular red with few claims to subtlety. But the wine is smoother and not as tight as the '95, of which few cases were made. Worth sampling, for a taste of what the future may hold. $24.

1995 Pindar Syrah
Dense, husky and brooding, it's not an easy friend. The wine, does, however show potential for what comes after. $24.

Zinfandel

The spicy, robust red zinfandels of California set the standard. Don't confuse them with the sweetish, fizzy, lightly fruity white zinfandel, a style whose blushing popularity for a time overtook the original's. Try a zinfandel from Cline, Rabbit Ridge, Ravenswood, Ridge, St. Francis or Turley.

One Long Island producer has tried zinfandel, which does better in a hotter climate.

1998 Pugliese Zinfandel
Fruity and straightforward, with an affinity for red meat. The wine is fun. $15.

1996 Pugliese Zinfandel
Medium-bodied, blunt, with some of the varietal's spiciness. $15.

Red Blends

You could argue persuasively that the best reds produced on Long Island aren't merlot or cabernet sauvignon or cabernet franc, but the unions made among them.

Producers have followed the Bordeaux model with success. The blends also encompass lower-end wines that show up best at a barbecue or a picnic.

1997 Bedell Cupola
Ripe, rich and balanced. A very satisfying alliance of 70 percent cabernet sauvignon, 20 percent cabernet franc and 10 percent merlot. Suggestions of blueberry, plum, and even more of cassis. Minty notes and just enough oak. $28.

1995 Bedell Cupola
Big and fruity, with lots of plum. The wine at first seems Californian. But it evolves toward the French and has a powerful personality. Expect a decent life span. This blend includes 65 percent cabernet sauvignon. $25.

1994 Bedell Cupola
The first Bedell Cupola and a very good, very smooth debut. Lighter in style than succeeding vintages. $25.

Bedell Main Road Red
Mix of merlot and cabernet sauvignon. The label portrays a vintage pick-up truck. It's far from a bumpy ride. $10.

1995 Bidwell Claret
The newest combination from the brothers Bidwell. A full-bodied production in which you'll detect berry and chocolate notes. Accessible now. But a year or two in the bottle

wouldn't hurt. Sold only at the winery. $35.

1999 Channing Daughters Fresh Red
Mostly merlot. A rustic wine that makes no demands. You could serve it slightly chilled and not upend the world. $12.

Duck Walk Gatsby Red
Love that name and that label. The wine is a lesser blend and a dry counterpart to Pindar's Sweet Scarlett. Not too smooth. But right with a slice of Sicilian on Daisy's dock. $11.

Duck Walk Windmill Red
Do you want garlic and anchovies on that pizza? Go ahead. $8.

Gristina Garnet
Flavorful, straightforward, three-way blend. Ready for red-sauced pasta. $10.

Hargrave Petit Chateau
Trés petit Bordeaux, mostly via merlot. $10.

Jamesport Island Rouge
At best, it hints at minor Beaujolais. $10.

1998 Jamesport Mélange de Trois
The newest edition of this play-

ful red, which has a trace of mint, and berry notes. About evenly divided between cabernet sauvignon and cabernet franc, with a splash of merlot. The wine is versatile and surprisingly soft. $24.

1994 Jamesport Mélange de Trois
A mouth-filler to be sampled with robust fare. Tasty blend, mostly cabernet franc. $16.

1993 Jamesport Mélange de Trois
Not as harmonious. $16.

Laurel Lake Wind Song Red
A lite tune. $8.

1997 Lenz Merlot-Cabernet Sauvignon Blend
The breakdown is 65-30, with the rest cabernet franc. Lighter, less tannic than the house's usual reds. Fruity and ready to drink. $17.

1997 Macari Bergen Road
Full-bodied, deep red: 55 percent cabernet sauvignon, 25 percent merlot, 16 percent cabernet franc, 4 percent malbec. A winning formula, with the majority grape's depth coming through. Hints of black currant and plum. Macari's top wine. Expect it to mature gracefully. $32.

Macari Vineyards Collina 48
Non-vintage, mainly merlot. Respectable table wine. If

Bergen Road is for steaks, this is for hamburgers. Good on its own scale. $10.

1997 Osprey's Dominion Flight
A well-structured red, 50 percent merlot, 45 percent cabernet sauvignon and 5 percent cabernet franc. The tannins have smoothed a bit and the bouquet is rich. Unfolding. $27.

Osprey's Dominion Richmond Creek Red
The modest alternative, suitable when you're unable to take Flight. $10.

1997 Palmer Select Reserve
Fine fruit and finesse are the hallmarks of this well-fashioned blend, which is mostly cabernet sauvignon. Cedar accents. Ample tannins. $25.

1995 Palmer Select Reserve
Excellent wine, with firm structure, plenty of plum and toasty oak. Still maturing. $25.

1993 Palmer Select Reserve
Mostly cabernet sauvignon, with about a third merlot and some cabernet franc. They harmonize well, buttressed by oak. Long finish. At its peak. $25.

1995 Paumanok Assemblage
The blend of this beauty is 55 percent cabernet sauvignon, 35 percent merlot, 10 percent cabernet franc. It puts the merit

in "meritage." Balanced, with lovely fruit, soft tannins, an undercurrent of oak. The best of the winery's blends, from a vintage meant to last. $24.

1993 Paumanok Assemblage
Harmonious, loaded with flavors of black cherry and blackberry, along with some mintiness. The fruit and tannins don't battle each other. Equal parts cabernet sauvignon and merlot, with 10 percent cabernet franc. $22.

1997 Paumanok Festival Red
A drink-tonight blend, full-bodied and good. $17.

Peconic Bay Local Flavor Red
Mostly cabernet franc. Definitely for the barbecue. The local image on the label is fun. $10.

Peconic Bay Classic Red
Also cabernet franc in the main. But past prime. $11.

1998 Pellegrini East End Select Red
Sturdy stuff made for hearty food. Cabernet sauvignon and merlot wrestling. Drink tonight. $10.

1997 Pellegrini East End Select Red
Medium-bodied, mostly merlot, with a hint of cherry. Drink today. $10.

1996 Pellegrini East End Select Red
Drink yesterday. $10.

1997 Pellegrini Vintner's Pride Encore
Big, serious ode to Bordeaux. Generous amounts of black fruit and firm tannins. It's 42 percent merlot, 38 percent cabernet sauvignon, 18 percent cabernet franc, with a couple of drops of petit verdot. As with the super '95, be patient. $29.

1995 Pellegrini Vintner's Pride Encore
Outstanding. A superior blend. Bigger and fuller than the '93. Rich, supple, elegant. Black fruit, a long finish, classic appeal. Expect it to improve for a decade or more. This Encore is 47 percent cabernet sauvignon, 39 percent merlot, 14 percent cabernet franc. Memorable. $34.

1994 Pellegrini Vintner's Pride Encore
Full-bodied and concentrated, balanced and supple. An earthy wine that continues to mature. Mostly cabernet sauvignon. $34.

1993 Pellegrini Vintner's Pride Encore
Black cherry is the lingering fruit in this exceedingly good wine. The '93 Encore is ready to perform now. $34.

1992 Pellegrini Vintner's Pride Encore
Fruity, supple, drinkable now. $34.

1997 Pindar Mythology
Finesse, depth, complexity are the hallmarks of Mythology from this vintage. The red blend keeps its history intact. Full-bodied but not as deep as the exceptional '95. $28.

1995 Pindar Mythology
Complex and inviting, showing Pindar's peak. Rich with the taste of berries and cherries, some oak and some spice. The finish is long and so should be the life of the wine. The impatient may drink it now. But earlier vintages should be sought while this one continues to grow. $37.

1994 Pindar Mythology
Ripe, full, recommended. The formula includes more petit verdot and malbec than the usual big grapes. $25.

Pindar Pythagoras
The new Pythagorean theorem is up-front. Made from young vines. A plummy, good red when you don't want anything big. Mainly cabernet franc. $12.

Pindar Sweet Scarlett
Semi-sweet, really. Tannins banished. Ho-hum. $9.

Pugliese Bella Domenica Red Table Wine
Uncomplicated blend of cabernet sauvignon and merlot. Have it slightly chilled. $8.

1998 Schneider Potato Barn Red
A second label from Schneider, made at Bedell. Forward, plump, drinkable combo of cabernet franc and 30 percent merlot. Not subtle, not bad. $15.

1997 Ternhaven Claret D'Alvah
The witty name underscores the winemaker's affection for the U.K. and the location of the vineyard on Alvah's Lane. The '97 is the fruitiest and most refined of the clarets to date. $24.

1996 Ternhaven Claret D'Alvah
Tannic and closed. $13.

1995 Ternhaven Claret D'Alvah
Not too smooth, but the fruit is good. $18.

1994 Ternhaven Claret D'Alvah
Tannic. $18.

Bubbling up on the North Fork.

Chapter 5

Sweet, Sparkling & More

Desserts and celebrations

This chapter is a blend of its own. It begins with those pretty-in-pink, salmon-shaded wines, called rosé or blush.

They're followed by sparkling wines, Long Island's bubbly relatives of Champagne. After these comes a series of dessert wines in varying styles, then, the high-alcohol, fortified wines. And it concludes with a category that, for reasons that will become immediately clear, is headed "Something Different."

Rosé and Blush

Rosé wines are made from red grapes. But the contact between the juice and the skin is minimal. So, they're the sort of red wines you can serve like white wines. Rosés may be semi-sweet or, in their best form, dry.

Blush wine is an American term. These sweetish wines are generally made from red grapes, and there's only slight contact between the grape juice and the skins.

Long Island wines in these categories cover a broad range. You can go from a wine reminiscent of a Provençal rosé to one that suggests sweetened mouthwash. It depends on whether the winery is making a wine for keeps or simply issuing an undemanding souvenir. Either way, these aren't meant to last long.

Bidwell Country Gardens
Blush Bouquet
Rosé for first-timers, stressing the sweet. $9.

1999 Channing Perrine
Fleur de la Terre Rosé
Fruity and refreshing, on its own or with light fare. $16.

1998 Corey Creek Rosé
An attractive, dry wine, with considerable body and lovely color. Notes of strawberry, golden apples, even tangerine in a flavorful dry rosé that's a hint of Provence. $10.

Duck Walk Windmill Blush
Rosy, with, yes, a cranberry note. $8.

1999 Gristina Rosé of
Cabernet Sauvignon
Crisp and fruity with hints of strawberry. Fresh and good. One in a series of tasty rosés from the producer. $13.

Hargrave Dune Blush
Pinot blanc meets pinot noir. Beached long ago. $6.

Hargrave Fleurette
Pinot noir is the grape that yields this non-vintage sipper. A lighthearted wine that's ready for a summer picnic. $10.

Jamesport Island Rosé
Easy to drink. That's it. $10.

2000 Laurel Lake Rosé
The first rosé under the new regime. It's fuller, more versatile and shows promise. $10.

1998 Laurel Lake Lake Rosé
Satisfactory fruit. Needs a chill. $10.

Laurel Lake
Wind Song Blush
Definitely blushing. Ice it. $8.

Loughlin South Bay Breeze
If you're a fan of white zinfandel, this playful bottle should do. $11.

**1999 Macari
Rosé d'Une Nuit**
Salmon-shaded, refreshing wine that says spring is here and summer is coming. Made with merlot, cabernet franc and cabernet sauvignon. $12.

**1998 Macari
Rosé d'Une Nuit**
Attractive dry wine made with cabernet franc. Good body at release. But past prime. $12.

**Osprey's Dominion
Twilight Blush**
Very sweet, with raspberry notes. $9.

Palmer Lighthouse Rosé
Very routine sipper. $10.

Palmer Sunrise, Sunset
More like sunset. Sweet. $8.

1999 Paumanok Vin Rosé
Refined, satisfying, easygoing, this rosé complements the cuisine of summer. Or have a slightly chilled glass on its own. $14.

1997 Paumanok Vin Rosé
A fruity wine, but the blush is off the rosé. $13.

1999 Peconic Bay Rosé of Merlot
Made entirely with merlot from young vines. Good vehicle for the grapes. Satisfactory and on the dry side. $13.

Peconic Bay Blush
Peachy, sweet, ho-hum. $9.

Pindar Spring Splendor
Sweet, cranberry qualities. $8.

Pindar Summer Blush
Minor. $9.

Pugliese Blush Table Wine
A little less minor. $8.

Ternhaven Harbor Rosé
Ternhaven cabernet sauvignon blended with upstate chardonnay. On the sweet side. $13.

1999 Wölffer Rosé
A dry, light and enticing wine, with lovely color and generous style. Strawberry notes, rose petals and a wonderfully dry finish. Tasty on its own or with casual fare. $11.

1998 Wölffer Rosé
A pleasant Provençal accent characterizes this rosé, which is fruity but not overly so. $11.

Sparkling Wines

In the realm of sparkling wine, there is Champagne and then there is everything else.

The great names of Champagne are many, Krug, Salon, Veuve Clicquot and the cuvée Dom Perignon among them. These are the wines of celebration.

But they aren't the only ones. Sparkling wines are well-made in Italy and the United States. Consider a pleasant prosecco or Asti, or any number of Californians, from labels such as Schramsberg, Iron Horse and, of course, Domaine Chandon, Maison Deutz, Mumm and Roederer Estate.

Carbon dioxide gas is a wonderful thing.

Jamesport Grand Cuvée
The blend is 75 percent chardonnay and 25 percent gamay noir. It's a light and refreshing sparkler, with a toasty note. $20.

Jamesport Blanc de Blanc
Up-front bubbles, ready to roll. It's the finale for this line of sparkler, which is pretty versatile. $17.

1994 Lenz Cuvée
Yeasty, toasty and elegant sparkling wine, made with 70 percent pinot noir and 30 percent chardonnay. Very dry. $30.

1993 Lenz Cuvée
Creamy, salmon-shaded, rich and full. Very dry blend in a blanc de noir style. Excellent. $30.

1992 Lenz Cuvée
Very dry, very bubbly, medium-bodied blend. $20.

1991 Lenz Cuvée
Medium-bodied, with hints of pear. $17.

1993 Lieb Blanc de Blanc
Bubbly, auspicious start, made entirely with pinot blanc grapes. Citrus notes. $20.

Macari Brut
The clean and attractive chardonnay-based méthode Champenoise number is fairly light, trés bubbly. $19.

1992 Palmer Brut
Crisp, dry sparkler, mostly pinot noir. Quite good. $20.

1997 Pindar Cuvée Rare
Dry, with yeasty notes and very good fruit and emphasis on the natural flavors. Made entirely with pinot meunier, which is reason enough to call it rare. $21.

1994 Pindar Cuvée Rare
Good sparkling wine, yeasty and very dry. Also, 100 percent

pinot meunier. $28.

**1998 Pugliese
Blanc de Blanc**
Chardonnay is the grape. A
light and subtle glass for local
toasting. $18.

**1997 Pugliese
Blanc de Blanc**
Versatile, light sparkler with
fine bubbles. Good for a summertime toast. $18.

**1996 Pugliese
Blanc de Blanc**
A light, very bubbly sparkling
wine made with chardonnay.
$17.

**1995 Pugliese
Blanc de Blanc**
Tiny bubbles and a toasty
touch. $17.

1998 Pugliese Blanc de Noir
Dry and quite French, with a
lovely salmon color. Made
entirely with pinot noir. $18.

1997 Pugliese Blanc de Noir
Refreshing, dry, satisfying bubbly that doesn't get too complicated. $18.

1996 Pugliese Blanc de Noir
Dry and direct, made with
pinot noir. Pretty salmon shade.
$18.

**1995 Pugliese
Blanc de Noir Nature**
All pinot noir. Dry, good. $18.

**1998 Pugliese
Sparkling Merlot**
The house's most playful wine,
with a spritzy, nostalgic quality.
It's fun. $18.

**1997 Pugliese
Sparkling Merlot**
A reminder of those sparklers
of your youth, grapey and not
too dry. $18.

**1996 Pugliese
Sparkling Merlot**
The vintages may change, but
the style really doesn't. $18.

**1995 Pugliese
Sparkling Merlot**
Exuberantly grapey. $18.

1996 Wölffer Cuvée
An elegant brut, complex and
satisfying. Harmonious, with
notes of hazelnut and apricot.
Minerally, with lively acidity.
$29.

1995 Wölffer Cuvée
Lean, clean, yeasty and bright.
Aging well. This cuvée marks a
return to the style of the winemaker's '93 sparkler. $28.

1994 Wölffer Cuvée
Creamy, yeasty, rich and fine in
its own way. Markedly different
from and heavier than what
came before and after. A good
sparkling wine. But you have to
like the style. $28.

Dessert Wines

Long Island produces a remarkable number of good dessert wines.

They're made with grapes that have been commercially frozen, to create a local ice wine, or with grapes that have been struck by botrytis cinerea, the "noble rot" that leads to the luscious wines of Sauternes.

These tend to be among the more expensive local wines, sold frequently in half-bottles. They aren't produced in large quantities. But a little goes far.

Bedell EIS
Intense and delectable, the non-vintage wine evokes the sweet stars of Germany. Made with frozen grapes. Dried fruit, particularly peach and apricot. Primarily riesling with some gewürztraminer. $27 half-bottle.

1998 Duck Walk Aphrodite
Gewürztraminer is the source of the wine in the cobalt blue bottle. The label is like a siren, beckoning lovers of apricot and peach. Quite sweet and free of complications. $28.

1997 Duck Walk Aphrodite
Uncomplicated late-harvest gewürztraminer. $28.

1996 Duck Walk Aphrodite
Spice, peach and a hazelnut accent mark this vintage. $28.

1995 Duck Walk Aphrodite
Honeysuckle and peach notes in a very sweet one that includes some riesling. Not too deep. $28.

1994 Duck Walk Aphrodite
Balanced, bright. Have it very chilled. $22.

1998 Macari Essencia
An aromatic and lush ice wine, made with one-third each of semillon, sauvignon blanc and viognier. Hints of apricot and honey rise from a wine that's both serious and playful. Chill a bit and enjoy the layers of flavor. $32 half-bottle.

1998 Jamesport Late Harvest Riesling
An astonishingly sweet and rich wine that measured 52 Brix at harvest. It has 25 percent residual sugar and 9 percent alcohol. Opulence in abundance, botrytis rampant. Touches of pear and vanilla. Expect it to mature for years. $44 half-bottle.

1998 Jamesport Semi-Glace
Made with frozen semillon, the wine has good acidity and the result is lean and sweet. More refreshing than seductive; a slim companion to the late-harvest riesling. $18 half-bottle.

**1996 Jamesport Late
Harvest Riesling**
Honeyed, ripe, with suggestions
of apricot. Concentrated
flavors. $25.

**1999 Palmer Select Late
Harvest Gewürztraminer**
Honeyed, ripe, well-balanced,
with good acidity, hints of apricot and a style reminiscent of
German dessert wines. Best
chilled and on its own.
$30 half-bottle.

**1996 Palmer Select Late
Harvest Gewürztraminer**
Lighter and crisper than the
'94. Attractive and perfumed.
$16 half-bottle.

**1994 Palmer Select Late
Harvest Gewürztraminer**
Wonderfully ripe, honeyed, aromatic, full of peach, with a
trace of spice. An exceptional
expression of the style.
$25 half-bottle.

**1998 Paumanok Late Harvest
Sauvignon Blanc**
Remarkable and decadently
ripe, this serious late-harvest
sauvignon blanc has wonderful
fruit. The winery's trademark
touches of quince and litchi
stop by. As close to Sauternes
as you'll find here, and even
better than the '97. Superb
dessert wine. $35 half-bottle.

**1997 Paumanok Late Harvest
Sauvignon Blanc**
Lovely, ripe and grand. A lush,
seductive evocation of France,
with aspects of peach and apricot, and a long finish.
Exemplary. $25 half-bottle.

**1994 Paumanok Late Harvest
Sauvignon Blanc**
Vivid, textured, cousin of
Sauternes. $25 half-bottle.

**1998 Paumanok Late Harvest
Riesling**
Fine acidity, richness, fragrance, with an accent of rose.
At first, it seems more
restrained than the '97. Then,
it supersedes its predecessor.
$19 half-bottle.

**1997 Paumanok Late Harvest
Riesling**
Rosy, very ripe, full of fruit.
Luscious and celebratory. $19
half-bottle.

**1994 Paumanok Late Harvest
Riesling**
The character of dried fruit,
apricot and peach threads
through. $16 half-bottle.

**1999 Peconic Bay
Riesling Ice Wine**
Concentrated, with fine mouth-
feel and enough acidity to hold
the sweetness in check. Very
good. $35 half-bottle.

1994 Peconic Bay Late Harvest Riesling
Fruity, undemanding. $13.

1998 Pellegrini Finale
The honeyed, lush wine has pleasing acidity and a diverting suggestion of orange peel. Versatile for a dessert wine. $25 half-bottle.

1997 Pellegrini Finale
Gilded and opulent, this is an intensely honeyed but still very refreshing ice wine. Made with frozen gewürztraminer and sauvignon blanc. The texture is almost viscous; the taste, a nimble balance of sweet and dry, with golden raisin and apricot qualities.
$25 half-bottle.

1994 Pellegrini Finale
Potent, full-bodied, luscious stuff. $25 half-bottle.

1993 Pellegrini Finale
Concentrated, opulent ice wine, suggesting apricots and golden raisins. $25 half-bottle.

1999 Pindar Johannisberg Riesling Ice Wine
Honeyed, with traces of tropical fruit. Rich stuff. $35 half-bottle.

1996 Pindar Johannisberg Riesling Ice Wine
Very rich, concentrated, with apricot notes. Serve slightly chilled. $35 half-bottle.

1999 Pugliese Late Harvest Gewürztraminer
Sweet and to the point, with a trace of spice. $10.

1999 Pugliese Late Harvest Riesling
Peach and apricot rise from this user-friendly wine. $10.

1998 Pugliese Late Harvest Riesling
Likable, rather delicate glass of sweetness. $10.

1998 Pugliese Late Harvest Niagara
You have to be a real fan to go for the niagara. Fruity and very sweet. $10.

1995 Pugliese Late Harvest Niagara
Not meant to age. $10.

1999 Wölffer Dessert Chardonnay
Refreshing and more restrained than many East End sweet wines. It has a hint of peach. Sold at the winery and in restaurants. $33 half-bottle.

Port

Port, the sweet and fortified wine, comes from the Douro Valley in Portugal. It exits the country from the city of Oporto.

Neutral spirits are added to wine midway through fermentation to make Port. That halts fermentation. The wine has lots of sweetness and more alcohol than your basic still wine.

There are vintage Ports, ruby Ports, tawny Ports, late-bottled vintage Ports, crusted Ports and more. Among the noble houses: Fonseca, Quinta do Noval and Taylor. On Long Island, a few wineries have gone the high-octane route.

1998 Jamesport "Anna" Pinot Blanc Port
This white Port wine is sweet and potent. There are suggestions of fig and cream. You could have it as an aperitif. Or open the bottle with dessert. $20.

Osprey's Dominion Port
A warmer to be sure. Some plum notes. Made with cabernet sauvignon. Cheese is the best accompaniment. $14.

1997 Pindar Cabernet Port
On the ruby side, sweet but with a definite kick later on. Aged two years in oak. $13 half bottle.

1994 Pindar Cabernet Port
Bracing, but with soft tannins. For cheese and walnuts. $13 half-bottle.

1992 Pindar Cabernet Port
Quite sweet, and made with the winery's customary vigor. $13 half-bottle.

1997 Pugliese Port Bello
Like wearing a very warm coat. Made with merlot and cabernet. Sweet. It goes with dessert or could be one by itself. $15 half-bottle.

1996 Pugliese Port Bello
A bracing, high-octane enterprise that's up-front and warming. Truly fortified, but personable. $15 half-bottle.

1999 Pugliese Raffaello White Port
Grapey warmer that actually doesn't mind a little chill. $15 half-bottle.

1998 Pugliese Raffaello White Port
It's 85 percent niagara, 15 percent muscat. Sweet and amply fortified as above. $15 half-bottle.

Something Different

Here are some local beverages made at the wineries that go beyond grapes. They have their place.

Bedell Raspberry
Many uses for this, from dessert wine to spritzer. Very sweet, high-octane. Made with fermented raspberry juice fortified with distilled grape juice. Boom. $10.

Duck Walk Blueberry Port
Made with wild Maine blueberries, this is an odd one to be sure. Sweet and boozy. $13 half-bottle.

Duck Walk Boysenberry
What you don't want to drink can go on the waffles or pancakes. $13.

Osprey's Dominion Cherry
The winery suggests you pair it with cheesecake. It could be a topping, too. $7.

Osprey's Dominion Peach
Make your own local Bellini. $7.

Osprey's Dominion Strawberry
Mix it with seltzer, have it on ice cream or give it straight to someone with a sweet tooth big as an elephant tusk. $7.

Osprey's Dominion Spice Wine
A microwavable wine for the grog moments. Red wine with cinnamon, cloves, and nutmeg. And those aren't the aromas; they're the ingredients. $8.

Winemaker Kip Bedell at work.

Chapter 6

Vine To Wine

How grapes become wine

For all its mysteries and romance, winemaking starts as farming. It begins with the soil. The elegant and symbolic vine is, finally, a tree with fruit. You plant it and go on from there.

What makes the difference between an outstanding wine and a candidate for vinegar are the decision-making and the details; the specific grape variety, the precise location and type of soil, the exact climate. Which explains why Alex and Louisa Hargrave pioneered winemaking on the North Fork instead of in North Dakota.

"The soil is sandy loam and well-drained, and the roots don't get choked in clay," said Alex Hargrave, who explored locations as far afield as Oregon and upstate New York before planting in Cutchogue. "You can't imagine how hard it is to work in the Finger Lakes because of the hard soil and the shorter growing season. The 'microclimate' of the North Fork results in a season that's considerably longer than upstate's. The region is well-suited for red varietals such as merlot and cabernet franc."

The South Fork is cooler and generally more conducive to white wine grapes, though in recent vintages, notable reds have been made there.

Unusual local conditions, from the altitude of a vineyard to the effects of an ocean breeze, can spur grapes in unlikely areas. "We have a series of undulations running through the vineyard, and a variety of soil types and exposures," said Russell Hearn, consulting winemaker at Pellegrini Vineyards in Cutchogue. "Cabernet sauvignon should be on well-drained, sandier sites. Chardonnay or merlot can handle heavier soil types."

What matters even more than the composition of the soil and the rock is its capacity for drainage and water storage, so the roots have a reliable supply. Winemakers need to know a little geology before getting into chemistry and microbiology. Basically, when the soil is ultra-dry or overly wet, it won't be kind to grapes.

Once winemakers determine that a stretch of land will produce ripe grapes regularly, they may find that one part of the vineyard is very different from another. One side of a hill, one lot, one bloc, will be better or worse. Sloping land allows for warmer temperatures at the upper end. And the amount of sunlight and wind may not be the same throughout the vineyard. The union of soil and climate often makes wine from the same grape variety differ from region to region.

All merlots, for example, aren't identical. Taste merlots from France, Italy, California and Long Island and you'll frequently find significant differences. The land helps define why one Bordeaux can differ markedly from another that comes from nearby, or why a Barolo from one section of Piedmont will have qualities that another will not. Finding the right spot is a precise business. In France, where so many of the world's great wines are made, the soil that spurs the grapes might not be good for anything else. To paraphrase an old saying: If that soil were not the world's richest, it would be the poorest.

Fabulous wines come from grapes whose vines are planted in soils known for their chalkiness and their shale as well as sand. The soil is mineral-rich. And it steers the vine to concentrate on the fruit instead of the foliage.

Wine starts as a branch, or shoot, of a grapevine. It's cut and planted. Leaves and roots grow. It becomes a rootstock, a hardy branch of grapevine. The rootstock is selected for its strength. Growers acquire rootstocks, and cuttings of wine-producing vines are grafted onto them. These cuttings establish the grape variety.

Vitis vinifera is the native European species that yields the top wines, from chardonnay and riesling to cabernet sauvignon and pinot noir. Long Island is New York State's prime region for Vitis vinifera. Hybrids such as concord, catawba, seyval blanc and baco noir are more suited to the colder weather upstate. Vinifera is hardy, too. Witness the success of riesling in cooler areas.

But more than a century ago, vineyards in France were ruined by phylloxera, a louse from native American plants that dined on vinifera roots. Phylloxera also wiped out California vineyards in the 1880s. Some native American species resisted phylloxera, however, and an effective way to combat the louse was found: grafting vinifera onto rootstock with the immunity. Most wine-producing vines now are the result of this marriage.

Rootstocks are planted in spring. Grafting is summertime work. By the following spring, there should be growth from the grafted bud. The plant is trimmed and protected to ensure growth of the bud and to direct the growth upward. Depending on the location, three to seven years will pass before the vineyard produces a harvestable crop from those vines. Each grapevine has its own cycle for maturation.

Winemakers use "canopy management," or trimming of the vine into its most effective shape. There are several methods of pruning and training a vine. The systems are geared to spread leaves and, accordingly, cut back shade and capture sunlight. What's used depends on the grape. Vinifera grapes have "an upright growth habit," said Louisa Hargrave. "Hybrids drape downward."

Ripeness Is All

To make excellent wine, you need excellent fruit. "It is the most crucial component," said Charles Massoud of Paumanok Vineyards in Aquebogue. "The old phrase is 'The wine is made in the vineyard, not in the winery.' If you don't make mistakes, you can make very good wine. But you're not going to be able to improve on the quality of the fruit."

The grape on the vine ripens in stages.

Basically, the grape becomes larger and heavier, accumulates sugars, reduces acids, forms its tannins and aromas, and changes skin color. Each type of grape, depending on climate, has a particular time to be picked. Chardonnay is early; cabernet sauvignon, late. Long Island requires an unusually long and sunny stretch to produce first-rate cabernet sauvignon. An earlier-ripening red, such as merlot, has an advantage on the North and South Forks.

From the time the berries form until ripening begins could be called the opening act. Ripening starts, the fruit swells and the colors change. White grapes go from green to yellow, and black grapes from green to light red and then dark red. The sugar in the grapes rises quickly.

That's followed by ripening to full maturity, as the grape continues to swell, heighten its sugar and lose acidity. There are times when the grape stays on the vine beyond maturation. The overripe grape, a source of dessert wines, is more concentrated in sugar.

Harvesting starts when the winemaker decides that the correct ratio of acid and sugar in the grapes has been achieved. A grape can offer different degrees of tartness and sweetness. It will gain sugar through photosynthesis during a sunny growing season, such as those in 1995 and 1997 on Long Island. Without sufficient sun and heat, grapes won't ripen properly and the wines won't be as good. Many of the 1996 Long Island reds provide local evidence. Maximum ripeness is the goal and the grapes are monitored every day.

Grapes are harvested primarily by machine. But some producers continue to harvest by hand, especially for dessert wines. Sometimes, grapes are harvested when frozen, for sweet "ice wine." On Long Island, ice wines are made from grapes that are frozen commercially.

Crushing and Pressing

When the harvested grapes rest on each other, they produce free-run juice, or juice extracted without machine pressing. The crush and the press follow. The crush part of the process involves removing stems and breaking skins, releasing the pulp, allowing the juices to flow. The crusher and destemmer are similar to a strainer, with paddles separating the grapes and stems.

Pressing has become a gentler process than it used to be. For white wines, skins and juice are separated in the presser. If the skins and juice aren't separated immediately, the skin may impart additional flavor to white wines. For rosé wine, the juice has brief contact with the dark skins.

To make red wine, the juice, skins, pulp and seeds are piped into fermentation tanks. Red wine stays with the skins through fermentation and occasionally beyond. That gives the wine color. The skins have phenolics, compounds that can make the wine astringent. Fermentation containers are stainless steel temperature-controlled tanks or oak barrels.

Grapes develop natural yeasts. They may be airborne in the vineyard and on the bloom on the grape's skin. Yeast contacts the sugars in the juice, and the sugars are converted to alcohol and carbon dioxide. Winemakers add selected strains of cultured yeast to the mixture because natural yeasts may be inconsistent. The special yeasts bring a particular quality to the wine, such as aromatics.

The fermenting juice is monitored constantly, until the sugar has been transformed to alcohol. A hydrometer is used to measure the decreasing sugar. The alcohol level goes up. The yeasts perish. Coolants in the steel tanks regulate temperatures, enabling the producer to control the fermentation rate.

In still wines, the carbon dioxide goes into the air; for sparkling wines, the carbon dioxide stays in. Most of the sparklers are made via a second fermentation, in tank or bottle. A sugar-yeast combination is added.

During red wine fermentation, skins and seeds bubble to the surface. The resulting "cap" is punched down manually or from a stream of juice pumped up from the tank's bottom.

If the winery is producing a fortified wine, such as Port, fermentation is halted when neutral spirits are added. This jars the yeasts while the wine is still sweet to increase the alcohol.

After fermentation for still wine, a process that can last weeks, comes clarification, letting the wine settle and transferring it to another barrel or tank. The goal is to remove solids. The longer the wine can be left to settle, the less maneuvering has to occur later.

Sediment, mostly from the yeast, is called the "lees." Some wines intentionally are given more contact with the lees to heighten their flavor.

Fine-Tuning

Malolactic fermentation is a secondary fermentation for reds and some whites to soften the wine. It converts the assertive malic acid to weaker lactic acid and carbon dioxide. This fermentation is considered helpful when there's too much acidity.

Chaptalization is another action used to shape wine in cooler climates. Sugar is added to make up for underripe grapes and thereby produce more alcohol. In warmer regions, tartaric acid may be added to compensate for lower natural acidity.

The wine also may be filtered before bottling by passing it through ducts or pores that act as strainers and isolate particles. But not all wines are filtered.

Fining, using a substance such as beaten egg whites or gelatins to attract solids, is another technique to clarify wines.

Some wines will age; some will go to the bottling line. White wines typically are bottled within a year. Red wines usually aren't. The winemaker decides how long to keep the wine in the tanks or the oak barrels. American and French oak barrels are used; some are old barrels, some new. Each will impart a particular quality. Every winery has its own approach with each wine and each vintage. It can be weeks or years before the wine goes into the bottle.

"This is three different businesses," said Joel Lauber, former owner of Corey Creek Vineyards in Southold. "You have to grow the fruit, and you can fail there easily. Then, you have to make decent wine. Then you have to market it. And you can't do it two-out-of-three."

White wines range from pale straw to golden; reds, from purplish to brick red and near-black.

Chapter 7

The Match Game

What goes with what?

Red or white? It's a question to make you blush. There have been essays, tracts and books written about whether it's criminal to serve a fish with red wine or beef with white. History doubtless records wars of the rosés, too.

The main thing to keep in mind is whether you like the flavor that results. Wine and food have their own specific tastes; when they come together, a third taste is created. Also, whether you're thinking about poaching a salmon or opening a can of tuna, remember that whatever sauce or

dressing ends up on the entrée can have more impact on the appropriateness of the wine you drink than the properties of the main ingredient itself.

All this inevitably leads to shorthand, if only to make pairings easier. And any quick reference, whether it's a star rating for a restaurant or a thumbs-up for a movie, can be seen as strict codification. So, it's best to view charts and ratings as general references, not precise directives. There is no meal that calls for a solitary, perfect wine. The perfect wine is a product of the imagination, not the chef. Plenty of different wines are terrific with plenty of different dishes.

It's also true, however, that some foods have a head-on run-in with some wines. You wouldn't want to have spicy, up-front barbecue with a mild white, or subtle sole in butter sauce with a big, tannic red. Have a few walnuts, which are tannic in themselves, with an astringent wine, such as an immature cabernet sauvignon, and you'll definitely pucker up, though not in a romantic way.

The most sensible way to think about matching food and wine is in a straightforward manner. Decide on the body and the texture of the food and of the wine, and the flavors. For example: Consider whether the dish is salty or sweet, rich or not. Or whether it's highly spiced, awash in cream sauce, smoky, peppery or plain. Then, decide whether you want what's in the glass to be similar to or in contrast with what's on the plate.

If you're planning a multi-course meal with several wines, the traditional approach is to serve wines that are lighter in body and less complicated in taste before heavyweight, complex wines. White wines precede reds. Dry wines arrive before sweet ones. Young is drunk before old. And you can enjoy a light red before a full-bodied white without causing an international crisis. You don't have to uncork a different bottle with every course. A lot of meals go well with just a white wine, or a red or a rosé.

Certain wines do have an all-purpose role, and that accounts in part for their popularity. Beaujolais, the fruity red, is a dependable bottle on the wine list. Accessible, soft merlot has soared because of its easy-drinking quality and versatility. Pinot grigio does the same for whites, along with sauvignon blanc and some rieslings. Champagne and other sparkling wines are festive and excellent before you get to the appetizers.

Friends and Enemies

But all wines don't harmonize with all foods. If you drank an acidic wine with a vinegary salad, the taste would be wiped out. Fruit vinegars, however, may not do the same. Sparkling wine combats saltiness. Mayonnaise and chocolates upend wine. It has been argued for years that an artichoke can wreck wine. Biochemistry is cited. To which the equally acceptable replies may be quiet agreement or "So, what?"

It is known that protein helps break down tannin, the preservative compound in grape skins that gives red wine astringency and a longer life. It follows that a steak tastes great with a full-bodied cabernet sauvignon. Milk also has protein that lessens the tannin in red wine. This is one of the reasons that cheese goes so readily with red wine. And why you can have a cheeseburger with your favorite red, too. High tannin and acidity help cut the richness of a dish.

Wine and food matches that at first might not seem sensible can turn out to be memorable. At the pricey end, devotees of recklessly rich foie gras will find a ripe partner for it with the elegant sweetness of Sauternes. If you're into the third or fourth shared dish at a Chinese feast, the aromatic and floral qualities of gewürztraminer will contentedly take part.

Seafood and lamb are among the entrées-in-waiting that call for contrasts. When preparing seafood, you'll note that what's first-rate with fish in cream sauce will not be with grilled fish. And what appears flawless with delicate, firm Dover sole won't necessarily be perfect with oily bluefish. The wine that has an affinity with lightly sauced salmon may not be enamored with the smoked variety.

Seasoning can mask the primary characteristics of a dish, whether fish or meat.

Compatibility between foods and wines stems from geography, too. When you sample the deep flavors and wintry cooking of Piedmontese cuisine, it's not surprising to see that Barolos and Barbarescos are apropos. For the lighter foods of this region of northern Italy, a dolcetto is a mainstay. Similarly, choucroute, the soulful combination of sauerkraut and pork, naturally links up with an Alsatian riesling. And paella marries well with Rioja. On Long

Island, the local merlots and duckling are a popular pairing. So are the lobsters and the chardonnays.

Affinities

Following are some suggestions for matching wines and foods. The wines aren't limited to those produced on Long Island. But all are available here.

Antipasti
Pinot grigio, Orvieto, dolcetto, Barbera

Artichokes
Sauvignon/fumé blanc

Asparagus
Riesling, chenin blanc

Barbecue
Zinfandel, shiraz, Barbera

Roast beef
Cabernet sauvignon, merlot, zinfandel

Beef brisket
Cabernet sauvignon

Beef stew
Cabernet sauvignon, Rhône Valley reds

Bluefish
Light merlot, sauvignon/fumé blanc

Caesar salad
Sauvignon/fumé blanc

Cajun dishes
Sauvignon/fumé blanc, gamay, Beaujolais

Carpaccio
Light reds

Caviar
Sparkling wines

Chicken pot pie
Riesling, pinot blanc

Fried chicken
Light chardonnay, gamay, Beaujolais

Grilled chicken
Chardonnay, Chianti, merlot

Roast chicken
Light merlot, gamay

Chili
Zinfandel, rosé, gamay

Chinese dishes
Sauvignon/fumé blanc, gewürztraminer, riesling

Fried clams
Light chardonnay

Raw clams
Pinot grigio

Cod
Chardonnay

Cold cuts
Fruity reds, rosé

Crab cakes
Sauvignon/fumé blanc, dry riesling

Soft-shell crab
Sauvignon/fumé blanc, pinot blanc

Curry
Gewürztraminer, sauvignon/fumé blanc

Duck with fruit sauce
Chardonnay, zinfandel

Roast duck
Cabernet sauvignon, merlot, pinot noir, zinfandel

Eggplant Parmigiana
Chianti, dolcetto

Eggs
Fruity whites, light reds

Filet mignon
Merlot, red Burgundy

Fish and chips
Sauvignon/fumé blanc

Fish stew
Pinot blanc, rosé, light merlot

Flounder
Chardonnay, pinot blanc, sauvignon/fumé blanc

Foie gras
Sauternes, late-harvest sauvignon/fumé blanc

Game
Barolo, red Burgundy, Rhône reds, zinfandel, pinot noir

Greek dishes
Sauvignon/fumé blanc

Halibut
Chardonnay, pinot grigio

Ham
Fruity riesling, rosé, light chardonnay

Hamburgers
Zinfandel, merlot, Chianti

Hot dogs
Beaujolais, gamay, fruity riesling

Indian dishes
Gewürztraminer, gamay

Japanese dishes
Light chardonnay, chenin blanc, sauvignon/fumé blanc

Roast lamb
Red Bordeaux, cabernet sauvignon, merlot, zinfandel

Lasagna
Chianti, Barbera, merlot

Liver
Cabernet sauvignon, merlot

Baked/stuffed lobster
Chardonnay, sauvignon/fumé blanc

Broiled lobster
Chardonnay, sparkling wine

Steamed lobster
White Burgundy, chardonnay

Meat loaf
Zinfandel, merlot

Mexican dishes
Fruity whites and reds, rosé

Monkfish
Chardonnay

Mushrooms
Chianti, Barolo, merlot

Steamed mussels
Pinot blanc, chenin blanc, chardonnay

Onion soup
Beaujolais, gamay

Oysters
Chablis, Sancerre, sauvignon/fumé blanc

Paella
Red or white Rioja

Pasta with cream sauce
Chardonnay

Pasta with meat sauce
Barbera, Chianti, dolcetto, merlot

Pasta with pesto
Chardonnay

Pasta with seafood/red sauce
Light merlot

Pasta with seafood/white sauce
Verdicchio, pinot grigio, light chardonnay

Pasta with tomato sauce
Cabernet franc, Barbera

Pasta with vegetables
Fruity whites

Stuffed peppers
Rosé, light reds

Pizza
Chianti, shiraz, red
Rioja, merlot

Pork chops
Chardonnay, merlot

Roast pork
Riesling, light reds

Pot roast
Zinfandel, Beaujolais

Porterhouse steak
Cabernet sauvignon,
zinfandel, shiraz

Prime rib
Cabernet sauvignon,
Rhône Valley reds

Quiche
Pinot blanc, riesling

Rabbit
Merlot, cabernet
franc

Grilled salmon
Chardonnay, rosé,
merlot, pinot noir

Poached salmon
Sauvignon/fumé
blanc, riesling

Scallops
Gewürztraminer,
fruity riesling,
sauvignon/fumé
blanc

Shrimp cocktail
Chenin blanc, pinot
blanc

Grilled shrimp
Sauvignon/fumé
blanc

Sirloin steak
Cabernet sauvi-
gnon, merlot,
Barolo

Smoked fish
Sancerre, gewürz-
traminer, muscat,
sauvignon/fumé
blanc

Snapper
Sauvignon/fumé
blanc, chardonnay

Sole
Pinot blanc, sauvi-
gnon/fumé blanc,
chenin blanc

Striped bass
Chardonnay

Sushi
Chenin blanc,
riesling,
gewürztraminer

Swordfish
Chardonnay,
light reds

Thai dishes
Chenin blanc, pinot
grigio, rosé, light
merlot

Trout
Riesling, light
whites

Tuna
Fruity whites,
merlot

Turkey
Dry riesling, pinot
noir, zinfandel,
light red Burgundy

Veal chops
Cabernet sauvignon,
merlot

Veal piccata
Pinot blanc, sauvi-
gnon/fumé blanc

Roast veal
Chardonnay,
sauvignon/fumé
blanc, pinot noir

Venison
Cabernet sauvignon,
Rhône Valley reds,
Barolo, zinfandel

Vietnamese dishes
Gewürztraminer,
rosé

The cellar at Wölffer Estate, where red wines and barrel-fermented chardonnays are kept in a temperature and humidity controlled environment.

Chapter 8

Swirl, Sniff, Spit

Testing is detective work

Wine tastings could make you spit. Then again, that's something you have to do, unless you want to turn horizontal at a vertical tasting. There's a difference between wine tasting and wine swallowing. And there are reasons for all that sniffing and swirling. You're gathering information, finding how a good wine reveals itself and what qualities it possesses. It can be both entertaining and educational.

There are different kinds of tastings. In a horizontal

tasting, you sample wines of the same vintage from different producers; for example, a dozen Long Island merlots from 1993. A vertical tasting compares different vintages of the same wine; for example, Lenz Merlot, from 1988 to 1995.

An enjoyable and lighthearted introductory tasting could bring together different grape varieties, or the same grapes from different regions, allowing you to determine similarities and differences. For example, you could sample a chardonnay, a riesling, a gewürztraminer, and a sauvignon blanc, or a cabernet sauvignon, a pinot noir, a merlot and a gamay. Then, examine chardonnays only, from Burgundy, California, Australia and Italy, or merlots from California, Pomerol or Saint-Émilion, Washington State and Long Island.

Of course, you don't have to go through all the formalities of a tasting to enjoy wine. And you shouldn't bother applying those techniques to wines that are routine.

Consider six general categories for white wines and four for reds, along with one for fortified wines, which are higher-alcohol wines to which spirits have been added.

Styles of Wine

Aromatic white wines:
These wines have floral, fruity and herbal qualities. They include muscat, sauvignon/fumé blanc, gewürztraminer, pinot grigio and some German riesling.

Light, dry white wines:
They're mild wines, and could be seen as all-purpose. You may enjoy them as aperitifs, with a variety of foods, or for a casual drink. Among these wines are pinot blanc, Verdicchio, Orvieto, Muscadet and some Chablis.

Medium-bodied, dry white wines:
Such wines have more varietal character; you know you're drinking a chardonnay or a riesling. Some of these are Chablis, Chassagne-Montrachet, some U.S. chardonnay, Alsatian riesling, and Greco di Tufo.

Full-bodied, dry white wines:
These wines have more complexity, greater texture. The great whites such as Le Montrachet and Corton-Charlemagne are examples, as are Meursault, Graves and top U.S. chardonnay.

Fruity, off-dry white wines:
These display some sweetness.
They're very appealing, light,
and pair well with food. Good
on their own, too. Johannisberg
riesling, chenin blanc, Müller-
Thurgau, gray riesling and
Vouvray are indicative.

Sweet:
Dessert wines, with the ultimate
ripeness of the fruit, and high
sugar content. Trockenbeeren-
auslese and Beerenauslese from
Germany. Sauternes and Barsac
from France, ice wines and late-
harvest U.S. varieties.

Light, fruity red wines:
They're young and have a
grapey quality. Tannin is low.
Beaujolais and Beaujolais
Nouveau are typical. Also dol-
cetto, gamay, Grenache and
Valpolicella.

Medium-body, dry red wines:
These display more varietal
character and texture. Merlot,
cabernet franc, Chianti
Classico, Côtes-du-Rhône, some
Burgundies and some U.S.

cabernet sauvignon fit the
description.

Full-bodied, dry red wines:
They have deeper flavors and
more texture. For full-bodied
dry reds, consider syrah/shiraz,
zinfandel, some Rioja, some
Bordeaux and Burgundies,
and certain U.S. cabernet
sauvignon.

Big, powerful, dry red wines:
Here are the long-lived, rich,
tannic and complex wines. The
top Bordeaux and Burgundies,
Côte-Rôtie and Hermitage, also
from France. Barolo and Brunello
di Montalcino from Italy.

Fortified wines:
A fortified wine results when
brandy or neutral spirits are
added to increase the wine's
alcohol content. Some fortified
wines have more than 20 percent alcohol compared with
between 7 and 14 percent for
dry, table wine. Fortified wines
include Port, Sherry, Madeira,
Malaga and Marsala.

Clues

In tasting these and other wines what matters is
whether you like the wine and are curious about what
attracts you, not whether your opinion coincides with that
of veteran tasters.

Nothing affects anyone's viewpoint, professional or
amateur, more than seeing the label. So, hold a blind tasting, which will allow for better judgment. And it pays to do
your tasting in a place with lighting that won't distort the

colors of the wine. There shouldn't be any foreign odors either, whether from food or cigarette smoke. They'll alter your ability to smell the wine. By the way, if you have a cold, postpone the tasting.

That's because so much of wine tasting actually is what you smell. Your palate is limited to sweet, sour, salty and bitter. But through the nose, you encounter thousands of aromas and flavors.

First, however, you ought to look at the wine to judge its clarity and texture. Wine should be bright and clear. Ideally it will have been poured into a thin, colorless, stemmed glass with a bowl that narrows at the rim. Such a glass will let you see the wine best, and will concentrate the aromas. A couple of ounces are enough.

Look into the glass from overhead and check the wine's color depth. Tilt your glass away, preferably against a white background. The action spreads the wine and enables you to observe color and viscosity, whether it's thin and watery or heavy, determined by how its film adheres to the sides of the glass. A light white wine won't have the texture of a honey-like dessert wine.

With white wines, you'll see a range of colors that go from pale yellow-green through straw to deeper yellow to deep gold. Or to brown, if the wine has gone bad.

With red wines, the colors move from purplish and ruby to brick red, to almost black. A little brown indicates the wine is older. Full-blown brown, however, isn't good for a red, either. It signals the wine is shot.

The colors indicate age and grape variety, important information about the wine you'll taste. They will help distinguish one wine from another. A young Beaujolais will have a purple shade; a vintage red Bordeaux will be brick red, with a tinge of mahogany on the edge. A great dessert wine such as a peak Sauternes becomes golden. Compare that with a very light German or Italian white, or a pale Graves.

Using Your Nose

Now, to the sniffing, which unveils many of the specific characteristics of the wine. Much of this is free association more than the application of rigorous criteria.

Take a whiff just after the wine is poured. Then swirl the wine and sniff again. You may get two different sensations. The swirling lets more oxygen get to the wine. And that aeration intensifies the smell, the aroma of the grape variety, the bouquet developed in the winemaking.

It spurs the release of those molecules of flavor on the surface. Vapors rise. Inhale. You're bringing the wine in contact, eventually, with the olfactory bulb. That's where the sensations make their impression. The wine is stimulating nerve cells.

You'll tell the difference quickly between, for example, a very fragrant riesling or a gewürztraminer and a chardonnay. Or between a plummy merlot and a spicy zinfandel.

Countless scents are found in wines. Professors at the University of California at Davis developed an "aroma wheel" that attempts to organize many of them, from earthy, fruity, chemical, floral, spicy and vegetative into more precise divisions, such as the type of fruit and the sort of flower.

In a red wine such as a Long Island merlot, you're apt to discover the fruity aromas of plum and berries, in cabernet sauvignon, perhaps cassis and cherries.

For a white wine such as a chardonnay, the fruity qualities may be pear, green apple or pineapple; for riesling, peach and apricot; gewürztraminer, litchi; and sauvignon blanc, lemon and grapefruit.

Sip the wine, letting some air in over it. Judge how the wine feels in the mouth. Slosh it around the palate. Swallow a bit. Then, exhale a little with nose and mouth. You'll learn how long the wine lingers.

Your tongue's tip detects sweetness; the middle, the fruit and tannin; the sides, acidity. You'll find whether the wine is soft or harsh, see whether the flavors are sustained, and gather impressions of the texture and the finish.

A chardonnay may suggest vanilla or butteriness; cabernet sauvignon, mint; zinfandel, black pepper; pinot noir, earthiness, as in mushrooms. You'll be sure whether the wine is sweet or dry, acidic or tannic, balanced or not. And you can start using terms like "crisp" for acidity or "flabby" for lack of it. Or skip the vocabulary part.

Drink or Hold

Wine is alive. You can enjoy its company young. You can grow old with it. Or you can kill it. And there are a lot of ways to commit vinicide. Actually, the best place to allow wine to age is a lot like a tomb: dark, cool and slightly damp. But more wine drinkers have hall closets than stone cellars.

Besides, most wines are made to be drunk earlier than later, if not immediately. Fruity, lighter wines are very popular, in part because the wine is ready to drink once it's bottled. And the wine usually is consumed soon after purchase. Long Island wines are no exception, even though a number of the reds have a decade or more of life in them.

So, unless you keep a bottle upright in the sun atop your boiler, it will likely survive until you drink it.

But if you plan to store a good bottle beyond six months to a year, you should think about where it ought to be, apart from within reach. Wine's biggest enemies are heat, light, and turbulence. Basically, you don't want to stash your best in the back seat of the car en route to a July Florida vacation while the kids are trying to poke a hole in the cork. The wine reacts to each stimulus.

Great wines age and mature well when they're stored on their sides at a temperature of 50 to 59 degrees Fahrenheit, with proper humidity, shielded from the sun that nurtured the grapes.

Wine is perishable. It's not wise, however, to put a bottle in your refrigerator for years. The maturing of wine can be retarded when it's resting place is too cold. Drop the temperature into the mid-20s, and lighter wines could get frosty.

If the spot is too warm, you'll be unintentionally speeding up the wine's life, but not improving it. Light also ages a wine prematurely. If the wine is in an environment pushing 80 degrees, the volatile compounds in the wine will be murdered, cooked away.

Overall, the temperature in the wine space shouldn't vary by more than about 20 degrees. Major changes in temperature can wreck wine.

And if it's not humid enough, the cork eventually will dry, allowing air to spoil the wine.

The reason wines are stored on their sides is to keep the cork moist and swollen, acting as a seal. Also, the bottle's neck is filled, so oxygen doesn't go in. Oxygen will ruin the wine. You also could angle the bottle to allow both the wine and the air bubble to touch the cork, leaving room for any expansion that occurs if the temperature changes significantly.

This applies to all wines in bottles with corks. Even Beaujolais Nouveau may benefit from a few months of proper storage. But the major good is to let potentially long-lived wines to mature steadily at their own pace, free from factors that either slow or speed the process.

There's no way to make wine develop quickly. You pay more for wines that have aging potential. So it makes sense to treat them carefully.

Storage

Racks and bins are the most common ways to store wine at home. If you have a house with a basement, the below-ground locale probably is your storage area. A dark closet also works. Pigeonhole systems, with a space for each bottle, and stacking systems in diamond-shaped bins are the most familiar.

Or, you could keep the wine in the producer's wooden or cardboard cases. But the humidity that nurtures the wine may cause cardboard to give way and wood to develop mold.

Temperature and humidity-controlled cabinets are increasingly popular, as interest in wine has grown and disposable income among buyers has risen. These units, which look like refrigerators, vary widely in size and price. They do provide the right conditions when nature doesn't. You're above-ground, too.

At Kedco Wine Storage in Farmingdale, N.Y., the cost of these typically begins at about $350 for a 24-bottle unit. A 700-bottle unit is about $3,000. Installing prefabricated rooms and converting existing rooms to wine cellars are among the company's projects, too.

If you're keeping fewer than 24 wines and plan to drink them within the next few months, you probably don't need an appliance-type unit. Stack the wine, and leave a bowl of water for humidity nearby.

At the other extreme, if you've got 1,000 bottles rolling around, some kind of orderly system will help. At least you'll be able to find the bottle you want. An alternative: companies that rent space in a temperature and humidity-controlled storage facility.

Long Lives

Wines that have long lives frequently are expensive. They're typically the tannic and concentrated reds. Long Island wines that are expected to last longer are red blends, such as Pindar's Mythology, Pellegrini's Encore, Paumanok's Assemblage and Palmer's Select Reserve, and merlots and cabernet sauvignons from years such as 1993 and 1995.

But since the industry is comparatively young, wines from the mid-1980s are considered the senior class.

Some reds from that period are drinking well now and have the potential to mature even more. Bedell's 1988 Reserve Merlot and Gristina's 1988 Cabernet Sauvignon are examples.

The top red Bordeaux have the most impressive record for longevity. Some can mature for 50 years or more. From a high quality vintage, expect red Bordeaux to last at least 20 years.

Stellar red Burgundies, such as those from Romanée-Conti, Musigny and Chambertin are generally more in the 15-year span. A Rhône star such as Côte-Rôtie or Hermitage may go longer. And the big Italian reds such as Barolo and Brunello di Montalcino may age 20-plus years. Cabernet sauvignon from California has shown aging potential, from producers such as Heitz and Robert Mondavi. But even these wineries are relatively young.

White wines that last are the greatest white Burgundies, such as Le Montrachet and Corton-Charlemagne. Dessert wines from late-harvest German rieslings to Sauternes age beautifully. So do the premier Champagnes, such as Moët & Chandon's Dom Perignon and Veuve Clicquot's La Grande Dame, and those of Krug, Bollinger and Salon.

Vintage Ports, from producers such as Fonseca, Taylor, and Quinta do Noval are known for their longevity.

Wine collecting itself is a hobby. What wine is collected in is akin to a booklover's shelves or a cigar smoker's humidor. You choose which items deserve the friendly confines, as opposed to the exile of inattention. If the bottle has a screw cap, don't worry about it.

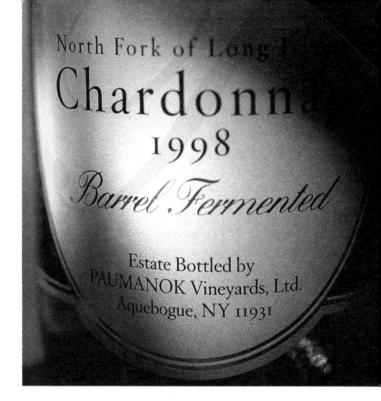

Chapter 9

What Are They Talking About?

A guide to winespeak

Trying to understand wine tasters at work can be similar to deconstructing dialogues on the upper levels of the Tower of Babel. It could lead you to drink.

The conversation starts getting strange when you find yourself among people describing wine the way you talk about a local politician: "dumb," "backward," "foxy," "flabby." Philosophers of language may spend years on the topic. But you want to know whether the wine is any good.

I've tried to avoid the jargon of wine writing in this book. Some technical terms, however, are in the text. What follows is a brief guide to winespeak.

Acetic—Vinegary. Not a good quality in taste or smell for any wine.

Acidity—How much acid is in a wine. From malic, tartaric and citric acid. Tartaric acid leads to the crisp flavor of some wines; malic, some fruitiness; citric, less. Other acids are produced in fermentation, too. As a wine ages, acidity dips.

Aging—In barrels, casks or bottles, this allows the wine time to improve. Aging often imparts a desired taste. The great red wines usually need aging to reach their peak. But most wines, especially whites, are ready to drink when they're released.

Aeration—Allowing air to reach the wine. You can do this by swirling it in a glass or by decanting the wine, pouring it from the bottle into another container.

American Viticultural Area—Or, AVA. It's a system of identification of U.S. wines by geography. Eighty-five percent of the grapes must be grown in the area to receive the designation. On Long Island, the Hamptons and the North Fork are two separate viticultural areas.

Ampelography—It's the word for the classification and study of grape varieties.

Angular—Used to describe young wines leaving a tart impression. Naturally, it means the wine isn't round.

Appley—Used in describing the aroma of a wine. Typical scents are green apple, which suggests young grapes, or ripe apple.

Aroma—The fragrance of the wine that's from the fruit. Typically, it will suggest either specific fruits or flowers, but also the wine's particular varietal characteristics and developments during fermentation and aging. Different from bouquet.

Austere—Short on fruit, due either to the compounds known as tannins or to acid.

Backward—An undeveloped wine.

Balance—A goal of winemakers is harmony so that none of the qualities of a wine, from fruit to tannin to sweetness to acidity, outweighs the others. In a balanced wine, the aroma wouldn't be stronger than the taste; the taste wouldn't wipe out the aroma.

Berry—The quality of ripe, sweet fruit in certain red wines, notably younger merlot and cabernet sauvignon.

Big—A description used for concentrated, rich, full-flavored wines. It's a compliment.

Blanc de blanc—White from white, meaning a sparkling wine made, for example, only from chardonnay rather than a blend of chardonnay and pinot noir.

Blanc de noir—Or, white wine from red grapes, often used for sparkling wines made with pinot noir. The skins of the grapes are removed before they color the wine.

Blanc fumé—Wine made with the sauvignon blanc grape. Also called fumé blanc.

Blending—Combining grape varieties or wines to make one wine that's greater than its parts.

Blush—A pale, rose-shaded wine that's made with red grapes.

Body—The texture, alcoholic content and mouth feel of the wine, whether full, medium or light. It's tactile. Consider the range between skim milk and heavy cream.

Botrytis cinerea—A mold that concentrates the sugar and flavor in the grape, often yielding outstanding dessert wines. It's also called "noble rot." All rot on grapes isn't.

Bouquet—The scents that arise from fermentation and aging in the barrel and the bottle. The combination of the alcohol and acids in the wine comes together in fermentation and aging in the bottle to form the bouquet, which typically may be a floral, fruity, or earthy. Complex bouquets develop in aging.

Breathe—Aeration. After the cork is removed and the wine is exposed to air, it starts to breathe. Better reds benefit from it. Sparkling wine goes flat.

Briary—Often used to describe red wines with bite, tannin and some spiciness. Zinfandels frequently earn the description.

Brix—The scale for measuring sugar content in grapes and wine, and the last name of the scientist who invented it.

Brut—Designation for the driest Champagnes and sparkling wines. Drier than "extra dry."

Bung—The plug used to seal the wine barrel. Of course, it goes into a bung hole.

Buttery—The scent and sometimes the taste of melted butter, invariably associated with rich chardonnays. It's a positive trait.

Canopy—The leaves and shoots of the grapevine.

Cap—The skin, seeds and stems that rise to the top of the juice during fermentation.

Cassis—The flavor of black currants, usually a reference point in describing cabernet sauvignon.

Chaptalization—The addition of sugar to the fermentation vat. Used to produce alcohol when grapes are underripe.

Chateau—In wineworld, used when referring to a vineyard or an estate. They're not all castles.

Chewy—Mouth-filling wines that are rich and intense. If not quite chewable, they still give the impression.

Citrus—As in grapefruit and lemon. Some white wines have citrus-like aroma and flavor.

Clone—A plant reproduced by graftings or cuttings to duplicate qualities of the original.

Closed—Refers to a young wine yet to show its potential

Crisp—The presence of refreshing balanced acidity with levels of flavor, depth, distinctions, subtleties.

Cru—French, meaning "growth," used as part of a vineyard's ranking in quality.

Crushing—Getting the juice out of the grape, typically with a crusher-stemmer. Grapes are broken and the juice, skin and seeds are separated from leaves and stems. Juice for white wine is separated from skins and seeds. To make red wine, the juice, skins and seeds go into the tanks together for fermentation.

Disgorgement—Removal of sediment from bottles of sparkling wine during the winemaking process. The sediment that has settled around the cork, because of its upside down positioning and regular turning by staff, is in the neck of the bottle. The neck is put in a solution to freeze the sediment, which exits when the cork is removed.

Dry—A wine that isn't sweet.

Dumb—A wine that's closed. This quality can last a long time.

Enology—The study of winemaking.

Esters—Compounds produced during fermentation and aging. They add complexity to the wine.

Fat—Used to describe a rich wine that doesn't overdo the acid.

Fermentation—How grape juice becomes wine. When yeast from the grapes or added by the winemaker triggers the process of turning sugar to alcohol. Fermentation takes place in small barrels, big vats, stainless steel tanks.

Filtration—A method to clarify wine and get rid of any solids. It can affect flavor in the wine.

Fining—Removing elements that make wines bitter or cloudy.

Finish—What stays on the palate after you've swallowed the wine. It refers to the taste and the texture of the wine. A lingering finish is desirable.

Flabby—Not the same as fat. A flabby wine lacks acidity and flavor. There must be a better word.

Flinty—Used in describing certain dry, white wines, which have a mineral aroma and taste suggesting flint. This does stretch the vocabulary.

Floral—Wines that have a hint of flowers in the aroma. Typically in white wines such as gewürztraminer and riesling.

Fortified—Describes wines to which neutral spirits or brandy have been added to increase the alcohol content. Port and Sherry, Madeira and Marsala are some fortified wines.

Forward—A wine that has matured early.

Foxy—Typically used describing the aroma and taste of wines made from hybrid grapes in the northeastern United States. They have an intensely grapey, musky character.

Free-run—The juice that flows before any pressure is applied to the grapes.

Fresh—Young, lively.

Fruity—It refers to the taste of the fruit from the grapes in the wine. A wine becomes less fruity as it ages.

Grafting—Attaching the bud shoot to the rootstock of grapevines.

Grapey—When a wine suggests the qualities of raw grapes.

Grassy—The scent of freshly cut grass, usually used in describing sauvignon blanc.

Gravelly—An earthy aroma.

Green—A wine from under-ripe grapes.

Hard—A very tannic or acidic wine. As in hard to drink.

Horizontal tasting—A tasting of wines from the same vintage but from different producers.

Hot—A wine with too much alcohol.

Ice wine—Dessert wine made with grapes frozen on the vine or commercially. The juice is concentrated, intense, with plenty of sugar and acid.

Lean—A wine that's short on fruit.

Leathery—Applied to tannic red wines that have a smell similar to leather, largely because of the wooden barrels in which they mature.

Lees—The sediment at the barrel's bottom after the wine has been pumped out. Wines sometimes are left "on the lees" to gain flavor.

Legs—The rivulets that go down the side of the glass after you've swirled the wine. Yes, they suggest the body of the wine.

Limpid—A clear, bright wine.

Lush—A very drinkable wine that's rich and fruity.

Maceration—The time grape juice remains in contact with skins and seeds.

Mouth-filling—Used to describe wines that seem to coat the mouth with flavors and textures.

Must—Crushed white grapes and juice after pressing; red grape juice with the skin, seeds and pulp after the crush and before fermentation.

Nose—The bouquet of fruity and flowery aromas in a wine.

Oaky—The term stems from wines that are aged in white oak barrels, made from wood in Europe and the United States. New oak barrels contribute toasty flavor and aroma to the wine. Traces of vanilla also may stem from oak. In some wines, oak becomes a dominant and not very beneficial factor; the wine is "overoaked." Red wines and chardonnays often are aged in oak.

Off-dry—Slight sweetness.

Open—A ready-to-drink wine.

Oxidation—Deterioration due to air exposure. The wine basically gets stale.

Phylloxera—A parasite that weakens the grapevine's roots. Vitis vinifera is very vulnerable, so these vines have been grafted onto native American rootstocks generally resistant to this plant louse.

Plonk—British slang for poor wine.

Pourriture noble—French term for botrytis cinerea.

Pruning—Cutting undesirable old growth to shape the vine for the most efficiency.

Punt—That indentation at the bottom of many wine bottles.

Racking—Transferring juice from tank to tank, or barrel to barrel, leaving behind the sediment. Not always a torturous process.

Residual sugar—Grape sugar unfermented or reintroduced to the wine.

Rootstock—The lower part of the root and buds used to reproduce the plant.

Round—A harmonious, graceful, balanced, full-bodied wine.

Sediment—Those deposits at the bottom of the wine bottle. Mainly with red wines as they age and tannins and pigments separate. White-wine sediment is almost colorless.

Soft—Refers to a fruity, easy-on-the-palate wine with comparatively low acid and tannin. In some wines, it's an attractive quality, but it also may suggest lack of balance. Used too much.

Sparkling wine—Wine with carbon dioxide bubbles. The carbon dioxide is either produced naturally or added. The style is perfected in Champagne.

Spicy—When a wine has the characteristics of spices, such as pepper or cinnamon. This may be from the oak of the barrel, or the grape variety. It doesn't necessarily suggest heat.

Steely—Lean and acidic, but well-balanced. Applies generally to white wines.

Still wine—Wine without carbon dioxide bubbles.

Sulfites—You see "contains sulfites" on wine labels. These are salts, from sulfurous acid. The information is on the label to state that sulfur dioxide entered into the winemaking. Some people have allergies to sulfites. For most, no source of concern.

Table wine—A still, unfortified wine.

Tannin—Tannins are compounds that act as preservatives and give wine a longer life. They come from the skins, stems and seeds, and give the wine structure. They're astringent and result in a puckery quality early on. Tannins soften during the aging process.

Tight—When a young wine is underdeveloped, it's tight.

Toasty—As in toasted bread. Wines kept in oak barrels with toasted interiors have this quality. It's most evident in chardonnays and in certain sparkling wines.

Ullage—When wine evaporates, space opens in the bottle or the barrel and causes exposure to air. That space is ullage. Winemakers minimize ullage by adding wine.

Varietal—A wine that uses its primary grape as its name. Varietal character means what a specific grape brings to the wine. You won't mistake cabernet sauvignon and gamay, chardonnay and gewürztraminer.

Vegetal—As in vegetables. Some wines do have suggestions of, for example, bell peppers. If there's too much of this quality, the wine isn't very good.

Velvety—Smooth.

Vertical tasting—A tasting of wines from the same winery but from different years.

Viniculture—Winemaking science.

Vintage—The year of the grape harvest from which the wine is made. Non-vintage wines used the grapes from more than one year.

Viticulture—The study of grapes and cultivating grapevines.

Vitis labrusca—A North American species of vines, primarily from the northeastern United States and Canada. Concord and catawba are from this species.

Vitis riparia—Also an American species of vines, used for rootstocks that resist phylloxera. Baco noir is from this species.

Vitis vinifera—The species of native European vines that yields the classic wines, from chardonnay and riesling to cabernet sauvignon and pinot noir. There are thousands of grapes in this species, which is planted worldwide and produces almost all the wine you drink.

Chapter 10

What to Buy Now

The vintages revisited

T he grapevine tells a vintage story. In any year, it can
be part comedy and part thriller. Or, depending on
the weather, a tale of terror. And when all goes
right: a classic.

The term "vintage" is from the French "vendage," or
harvest. It refers to the year in which the grapes are harvested, and to the wines that are made from those grapes.

In the United States, for a wine to be designated with a
vintage, 95 percent or more of the grapes used must have
been harvested in that year. When grapes from more than
one year go into a wine and no single harvest accounts for
at least 95 percent of the content, the result is a non-vintage wine.

Wine used to be kept in barrels instead of bottles. It wasn't until the late 1700s, when bottles were produced in roughly the shapes they are today, that extensive vintage dating began.

Since the size and quality of the grape harvest can vary significantly from year to year in regions from Bordeaux and Burgundy to the North Fork and the Hamptons, it's wise to note the vintage at least as a shorthand way of judging likely quality.

But assessments of wines typically are made extremely early. Often, it's only after blending that the evolving wine can be savored. Before that, you could say all wines are vintage wines. Blending grapes from different years is a common practice, especially when a winemaker wants to ensure that a particular wine has the same characteristics year after year.

So, consider the vintage a guide, suggesting which wines should be consumed now and which ones will mature well in the cellar or will last without much change in the hall closet.

That said, non-vintage wines more often than not are fine, too, bringing together more than one year's grapes to achieve a better overall result. Just because a wine is vintage-dated doesn't mean it's a better wine.

What matters more than the year is the bottle's content. From what has been deemed an excellent vintage, you may find wines in an extraordinarily broad range. And the price of a wine isn't necessarily a badge of quality. There are countless good, inexpensive wines and more costly wines that aren't satisfying at all.

Weather can level everything. Just ask any winemaker who has experienced a hurricane close to harvest time. Or a frost or heavy rains at an especially inopportune moment. A great summer in an area with younger vines still is likely to yield better wines than those coming out of a turbulent season in a revered growing region.

On the North Fork and in the Hamptons, vintages were quite good during the 1990s. About half of the decade's vintages produced recommended wines from almost every winery.

Long Island's wine industry is comparatively young, so it's difficult to gauge the life span of many of the region's wines. You can be sure that certain Bordeaux wines will last for decades, and mature as the years pass.

A Bordeaux that seems tight and tannic today will unveil

itself over time and show its depth and complexity. A Long Island wine may be ideal today or in five years. Whether it will be alive in 25 is a question only time will answer.

Based on recent tastings, the longest-lived Long Island wines are from 1988. White wines dating to 1997 continue to be sound choices. There have been years, usually the cooler ones, when the whites turned out better than the reds. Some sparkling and fortified wines from the 1991 and 1992 vintages have aged well.

What follows is a brief guide to Long Island vintages since the mid-1980s. Most of the wines from the early '80s are no longer available. You still may be able to find some reds produced from 1985 to 1988. But the Long Island wine on the market today is dominated by those produced from 1995 to 2000.

2000

A cool and rainy summer gave way to warm and sunny weather in September and October, rescuing what many winemakers believed was going to be a disappointing harvest. The early whites are good.

1999

Tropical storm Floyd paid a visit and trimmed the crop. But autumn was sunny, and the result was riper than expected grapes. The white wines so far have been respectable. Most of the reds have not been released yet.

1998

Warm, dry weather led to a good vintage for reds and whites. The reds generally are lighter-bodied and sometimes fruitier than the '97s. The whites are reliable and often very good.

1997

Among the top vintages of the decade. The harvest was about two weeks later than usual, thanks to lots of sun after Labor Day. The hot, dry weather allowed the fruit to reach maximum ripeness. Red blends, cabernet sauvignon and merlot benefited the most, and these concentrated wines are maturing well. Barrel-fermented chardonnays from this vintage currently set the local standard.

1996

A much lighter style of wine compared with the winners of the previous three years. Cool, rainy weather meant late harvesting, but the fruit still wasn't as ripe. The whites turned out much better than the reds, but you have to be selective to find very good ones. Overall, satisfactory at best.

1995

Lots of summer heat and warm, dry fall weather boosted the grapes. It was a big, outstanding crop. This remains a vintage to seek for full-bodied, first-rate red wines, comparable to and often better than those from 1993. The reserve reds and deluxe red blends are exceptional, yielding some of the finest wine produced in the region.

1994

The summer was warm, but the heat didn't last into September. Overall, a good vintage, with some similarities to 1995 and 1993. In certain cases, the wines actually were better than the '93s. But for the majority of the wineries, this year was a little dip between two peaks.

1993

For consistency and quality, the best vintage since 1988, whether for reds or whites. The concentrated reds continue to hold up very well. The year was defined by a hot, dry summer that wasn't overtaken by early September rains. Top levels of sugar and acid were present at harvest, which took place a couple of weeks earlier than usual because the grapes ripened so well in the consistent sunshine. The yields were lower than normal. Terrific wine, but not enough of it.

1992

A cool summer delayed the ripening of the grapes, in some varieties by more than a month. The result was better than expected, with high yields and satisfactory wines.

1991

Hurricane Bob made a dramatic cameo appearance. But the summer storm hit Long Island while the berries on the vine were hard. The fruit was pretty good, and so was the yield. Likewise, a surprising number of wines.

1990

The growing season was hot and wet. Autumn, warm and drier. A cold snap the previous fall didn't help. The yield was fairly small, with a very limited number of acceptable wines.

1989

Wet and cool. A hard year that still makes winemakers wince, considering how 1988 had elevated the industry's profile.

1988

This was the breakthrough vintage. The red wines were rich, with cabernet sauvignon and merlot still drinking well today. The season was long, hot and dry; the fruit, ripe.

1987

It was rainy late in the

season. The wines were forgettable.

1986

Few wines remain from this vintage, which was better for whites. A hot, dry season produced only serviceable-to-good wines.

1985

Hurricane Gloria treated the East End as rudely as it did the rest of Long Island. The surviving grapes yielded very modest wines.

Some Good Choices

Each winery has its specialties. Here's a selection of wines that will give you a representative taste. I've listed good buys; a sampling of the producer's best, or highlight, wines and, when applicable, something especially distinctive, different and worth a try. Call it serendipity.

Banfi Old Brookville Vineyards
Highlight: 1998 Chardonnay

Bedell Cellars
Highlights: 1997 Reserve Merlot, 1997 Cupola, 1997 Cabernet Sauvignon
Best Buy: Main Road Red
Serendipity: EIS dessert wine, 1999 Viognier

Bidwell Vineyards
Highlights: 1995 Merlot, 1997 Barrel-Fermented Chardonnay
Best Buy: 1999 White Riesling
Serendipity: 1995 Claret

Castello di Borghese-Hargrave Vineyard
Highlights: 1995 Pinot Noir "Le Noirien," 1997 Chardonnay Reserve, 1997 Merlot Reserve
Best Buy: Chardonette
Serendipity: 1998 Pinot Noir

Channing Daughters Winery
Highlights: 1998 Brick Kiln Chardonnay, 1999 Channing Perrine Sauvignon Blanc
Best Buy: 1999 Scuttlehole Chardonnay
Serendipity: 1998 Channing Perrine Riesling

Corey Creek Vineyards
Highlights: 1997 Merlot, 1998 Reserve Chardonnay
Best Buy: 1998 Rosé
Serendipity: 1998 Cabernet Franc

Duck Walk Vineyards
Highlights: 1995 Merlot Reserve, 1995 Cabernet Sauvignon
Best Buy: Southampton White
Serendipity: 1998 Aphrodite dessert wine

Dzugas Vineyards
Highlight: 1995 Chardonnay

**Galluccio Estate Vineyards-
Gristina Winery**
Highlights: 1995 Andy's Field
Cabernet Sauvignon, 1997
Andy's Field Merlot, 1998
Andy's Field Chardonnay
Best Buy: Garnet Red Blend
Serendipity: 1998 Pinot Noir

Jamesport Vineyards
Highlights: 1998 Late Harvest
Riesling, 1998 Mélange de
Trois, 1998 Natural Selection
Chardonnay
Best Buy: Island Blanc
Serendipity: 1998 Pinot Blanc
Port

Laurel Lake Vineyards
Highlights: 1997 Chardonnay
Reserve, 1998 Reserve
Cabernet Sauvignon
Best Buy: 2000 Lake Rosé
Serendipity: 1998 Riesling

The Lenz Winery
Highlights: 1994 Cuvée, 1996
Barrel-Fermented Chardonnay,
1997 Estate Selection Merlot
Best Buy: 1997 Chardonnay
Serendipity: 1997
Gewürztraminer

Lieb Family Cellars
Highlight: 1997 Merlot
Best Buy: 1998 Pinot Blanc
Serendipity: 1993 Blanc de
Blanc

Loughlin Vineyards
Highlight: 1999 Chardonnay
Reserve

Macari Vineyards
Highlights: 1997 Bergen Road,
1997 Barrel-Fermented
Chardonnay, 1997 Merlot
Best Buy: 1998 Viognier
Serendipity: 1998 Essencia
dessert wine

Martha Clara Vineyards
Highlights: 1999 Reserve
Chardonnay, 1999 Viognier,
1999 Riesling
Best Buy: 1999 Chardonnay
Serendipity: 1999 Semillon

Osprey's Dominion Winery
Highlights: 1997 Flight, 1997
Reserve Chardonnay
Best Buy: Regina Maris
Chardonnay
Serendipity: Gamay Noir

Palmer Vineyards
Highlights: 1997 Select
Reserve Red, 1997 Reserve
Chardonnay, 1998 Estate
Chardonnay
Best Buy: 1998 Pinot Blanc
Serendipity: 1999 Select Late
Harvest Gewürztraminer

Paumanok Vineyards
Highlights: 1995 Tuthills Lane
Limited Edition Cabernet
Sauvignon, 1995 Grand Vintage
Cabernet Sauvignon, 1998
Late-Harvest Sauvignon Blanc
Best Buy: Festival Chardonnay
Serendipity: 2000 Chenin Blanc

Peconic Bay Winery
Highlights: 1998 Riesling,
1999 Chardonnay
Best Buy: Local Flavor Red
Serendipity: 1999 Riesling
Ice Wine

Pellegrini Vineyards
Highlights: 1995 Vintner's
Pride Encore, 1995 Cabernet
Sauvignon, 1997 Vintner's
Pride Encore
Best Buy: 1997 Chardonnay
Serendipity: 1998 Vintner's
Pride Finale

Pindar Vineyards
Highlights: 1995 Reserve
Cabernet Sauvignon, 1997
Mythology, 1999 Johannisberg
Riesling Ice Wine
Best Buy: 1997 Peacock
Chardonnay
Serendipity: 1998 Gamay

Pugliese Vineyards
Highlights: 1998 Blanc de
Blanc, 1997 Blanc de Noir,
1999 Sangiovese
Best Buy: 1999 Raffaello
White Port
Serendipity: 1998 Sparkling
Merlot

Raphael
Highlight: 1997 Merlot

Schneider Vineyards
Highlights: 1997 Cabernet
Franc, 1997 Merlot,
1998 Chardonnay
Best Buy: 1998 Potato Barn Red

Ternhaven Cellars
Highlight: 1997 Merlot
Best Buy: Harbor Rosé
Serendipity: 1997 Claret
d'Alvah

**Wölffer Estate-Sagpond
Vineyards**
Highlights: 1997 Estate
Selection Merlot, 1997 Estate
Selection Chardonnay,
1997 Merlot
Best Buy: 1999 Dry Rosé
Serendipity: 1999 Dessert
Chardonnay

East Hampton Point: the view is dessert.

Chapter 11

Restaurant
Reservations

Where to dine in wine country

T he North Fork and the South Fork make up a table
setting that mixes country and city styles.
For many years, a weathered sign on the side of an
East End barn delivered the message "Potatoes Make the
Meal." For plenty of restaurants on the North Fork, they're
still a big part of dinner. The "terroir" is very hospitable to
country dining. Even the McDonald's in Mattituck has a
colonial touch, in the architecture if not the tray.

The eateries between Riverhead and Greenport, where
the majority of Long Island's wineries are located, are

dominated by informal, moderately priced establishments that specialize in pretty straightforward fare, with an emphasis on seafood, steaks and pasta. While there are a few pricier and more adventurous restaurants on the North Fork, not too many risk slashing themselves on the cutting edge.

One of the most enjoyable experiences you'll have could be simply buying a fruit pie at Briermere Farms and topping it with ice cream from Snowflake or The Magic Fountain. There it is: wine country à la mode.

The South Fork, of course, is very different, and not just because the best scoop is gelati from Sant Ambroeus. The Hamptons have long been one of the world's prime summertime playgrounds, and not solely because of the endless, white beaches.

Between Riverhead and Amagansett, chefs are more likely to bring New York City along with them in the back seat than offer a clam pie or a pristine, steamed lobster. But you'll find those, too. The price points begin down-to-earth and eventually go sky-high before reaching the astronomical. That said, however, in season the South Fork boasts some of the best cooking on Long Island. Off-season, it's not bad, either.

But the influence of the wineries on dining out on either fork has been surprisingly minimal. There have been a couple of spots over the years that have incorporated "vineyard" or "wine" in their names. But when it came to the menu, you could just as easily have been eating in Queens or Nassau. The one place that built its reputation concentrating on local produce and local wines, chef John C. Ross' North Fork Restaurant, closed in 2000. Ross still operates his barbecue and rotisserie business in Southold.

Among the better restaurants on the North Fork are Antares Cafe and Ile de Beauté in Greenport, The Seafood Barge in Southold, and the Modern Snack Bar in Aquebogue, where the homey style and seasonal dishes suit the Main Road mood.

In the Hamptons, some favorites are basilico and The Plaza Cafe in Southampton; Della Femina, The Palm at the Huntting Inn, Rowdy Hall, and East Hampton Point in East Hampton, and Station Road and Mirko's in Water Mill.

What follows is a selective guide to dining out during

Modern Snack Bar: don't forget the turnips.

your visit to wine country, with brief reviews of restaurants situated near the wineries. And, for dessert, a couple of ice cream emporiums are included because no trip is complete without a sugar cone or a sundae.

The establishments are listed by community. Prices are subject to change. As a form of shorthand, there's a rating system of $, $$ and $$$, going from inexpensive to moderate to expensive; or from $15 or less, to $25, and to more than that per person. The reviews reflect the restaurants' ratings as of autumn 2000.

Among the notable restaurants expected to open in wine country for the 2001 summer season are Star Room in Wainscott and George Martin in Southampton. The Seafood Barge in Southold has a new chef, but keeps the eatery's successful theme; and The Independent in Bridgehampton is slated to give way to Lure at Independent. The Wild Goose in Cutchogue is becoming even more imaginative.

Aquebogue

Meeting House Creek Inn
Meeting House Creek Road,
south of Route 25
631-722-4220.
You'll have a waterside perch
here, and the eatery is appealing
enough on a summer afternoon.
Casual and friendly, yes. But the
food can be erratic. Stick with
the simplest dishes of the day.
Maybe a blackened steak. $$

Modern Snack Bar
Main Road (Route 25)
631-722-3655.
This classic has been around
since the Truman Administra-
tion, and you'll like being in the
time capsule. Genial service,
unpretentious style. The
emphasis is old-fashioned
American food, from the meat
loaf to the roast turkey. In sea-
son, try the bay scallops. Also:
lobster salad, flounder, sauer-
braten. And be sure to take
home a quart of the great
mashed turnips; actually, take
two. They freeze well. $$

Amagansett

Estia
177 Main St.
631-267-6320
Popular all day, Estia com-
mences with blueberry pancakes and French toast, reaches
noon with a chicken salad club
or a BLT, and greets nightfall
with lots of well-sauced pasta.
And those pastas are good, the

flavors true. Crowded. An occa-
sional celebrity may walk in to
improve the scenery. $$

Gordon's
231 Main St.
631-267-3010
Predating nouveau riche and
nouvelle cuisine, Gordon's is a
dependable continental that
has been here since the
Kennedy-Nixon contest. Your
main course could be a juicy
veal chop, roast duckling or
beef Bordelaise; starters,
smoked salmon and escargots
Bourguignonne. The place is a
reminder of blazers and pearls,
though there's no longer a
dress code. Linger over a drink,
perhaps a Gibson. $$$

Mount Fuji
Montauk Highway (Route 27)
631-267-7600
Mount Fuji is never dormant.
Very splashy sushi, fresh and
prettily presented, is the lure.
Go with a group and sample
the "family boat" for three
heroic appetites, or the smaller
"love boat" to be shared by two.
Good sukiyaki, teriyaki, tempu-
ra. There's a branch in
Southampton. $$

Pacific East
415 Main St.
631-267-7770
A dramatic, white, high-ceiling
dining room is the setting for
dynamic, Pan Asian cuisine.
The restaurant is an offspring

of Pacific Time in Miami. You'll remember the Shanghai-roasted black bass, cedar-planked black cod, shrimp spring rolls, ginger-stuffed snapper and peppery duck. They segue west with a pink rack of lamb and snappy bananas Foster. Sometimes the mood of the place overdoses on cool, and staff members appear to be auditioning for other roles. But the food can be excellent. $$$

Bridgehampton

Bobby Van's
Main Street (Route 27-
Montauk Highway)
631-537-0950
Willie Morris and James Jones, John Knowles and Truman Capote, Irwin Shaw and Nelson Algren. They all must be wondering what happened to their old hangout. The Hamptons' lionized saloon-as-salon holds on to the name, but that's it. Now, it's a popular steak joint, where the crowd spills onto Main Street in season. Stick with dishes such as the porterhouse and sirloin steaks, roasted cod and seared tuna. Avoid anything that even sounds complicated. And, for old times sake, have a drink. $$$

Bridges
964 Bridgehampton-Sag
Harbor Tpke.
631-537-9105
A lively stop along the busy country road, Bridges is worth visiting for the Sunday gospel brunch as well as a respectable dinner. The southern-fried chicken competes with the meaty crab cakes; the sesame-crusted slab of tuna with a zesty five-spice trout entree. The pecan-and-macadamia nut pie is a rousing finale. $$

Candy Kitchen
Main Street (Route 27)
631-537-9885
Homemade ice cream, hamburgers, club sandwiches and other informalities are the staples. No real candy capital, unless you want a bar or two. $

Henry's
2495 Main St.
631-537-5665
Now, a bistro-style restaurant. This successor to the Bridgehampton Cafe and countless others at the address is awash in red, capped with a pressed-tin ceiling. Very pretty. Add a mahogany bar, cushy banquettes, pastel artwork, and enough buzz to wake the jaded. The raw bar is new; so's the ceviche du jour. Winning dishes include shrimp-and-salt cod cakes, grilled strip steak Bordelaise, and a delectable tarte Tatin. $$$

Independent
Main Street (Route 27)
631-537-5110
A Manhattan cast in an East
End setting. Go for the simplest
dishes and the show. On the
weekend, it's a noisy scene. $$$

95 School Street
95 School St.
631-537-5555
One of the East End's restau-
rants-for-all-seasons, as flavor-
ful in winter as in summer. It's
handsome, spare, pulsating.
And a hot address since 1993.
Braised short ribs with a
parsnip-potato puree; savory
chicken with Savoy cabbage,
bacon and red bliss potatoes; a
pan-roasted, dry-aged ribeye
steak with Gorgonzola sauce,
and gnocchi with capon, car-
doons and carrots are among
the treats. $$$

World Pie
Main Street (Route 27)
631-537-7999
Casual cuisine is the main
ingredient in this pie. Lobster
salad is good, as are some of
the designer pizzas including a
prosciutto-capped pie. Seared
tuna is an alternative. $$

Cutchogue

The Cutchogue Diner
Main Road (Route 25)
631-734-9056
Worth visiting just because of
its looks, the loosely Art Deco
eatery prepares basic stuff
morning, noon and night:
Belgian waffles, a roast turkey
salad sandwich, prime rib,
meat loaf, stuffed cabbage,
flounder. Local wines, home-
made desserts. $

The Wild Goose
4805 Depot Lane
631-734-4145
Hard by the railroad tracks in
the middle of wine country is
this little winner with plenty of
ambition. The menu changes
regularly. Perhaps it'll have the
smoked goose breast with fresh
figs and arugula; duck confit
with red onion marmalade;
roast pork with Calvados and
prune sauce; grilled ribeye steak
with a wine, mushroom and
shallot sauce, or the seared sea
scallops, with a coconut, cauli-
flower and artichoke puree. $$

East Hampton

Babette's
66 Newtown Lane
631-329-5377
A Hamptons feast, this likable
cafe could keep you nibbling
happily all day. Grilled polenta
pizza, club sandwiches, omelets,
cinnamon-swirl French toast. A
little later: hamburgers on

multi-grain buns, a Thai-seasoned vegetable stir fry. Maybe spot Billy Joel. $$

Blue Parrot
33A Main St.
631-324-3609
Polly-wanna-burger, or perhaps nachos grande. Casual food for before or after the movies. Keep it simple. $$

Cerulean Restaurant
143 Main St.
631-329-5550
A tropical breeze of a restaurant, with a terse, lively and ever-changing menu that brings you close to the beach. Mixed-media artwork and colorful fabrics have updated the former 1770 House restaurant. Some tantalizing dishes: monkfish foie gras with rice wine vinegar and green onions; halibut ceviche; mackerel or sardine escabeche; chilled pea soup with mint; crisp-skinned striped bass in Thai basil broth; yellowtail with a somen noodle cake, and panna cotta with marinated Bing cherries. Reservations are hotter than July. $$$

Della Femina
99 N. Main St.
631-329-6666
Jerry Della Femina, ad man extraordinaire, perfects getting attention. Here, he does so with food that has as much presence as the big, bald, goateed guy himself. The fellow who brought you the Ziploc talking finger and Joe Isuzu presides over a nightly gossip column-in-progress during high season. The restaurant attracts celebrities and anyone willing to part with odd lots of cash. Recommended: soy-glazed pork chop, summer tomato risotto, pan-roasted halibut, plum cobbler, Key lime cannoli. $$$

East Hampton Point
295 Three Mile Harbor Rd.
631-329-2875
You could count Long Island's first-rate waterside restaurants on one hand while wearing a mitten. Seductively summery, East Hampton Point arguably has the loveliest water view of all: a beautiful perch on Three Mile Harbor. The food is new American and consistently fine: oven-roasted veal chop, grilled steak, roast chicken, corn-and-shellfish chowder, all done with flair. $$$

The Farmhouse
341 Pantigo Rd.
(Route 27)
631-324-8585
The Farmhouse is carefully tended, in image and in food. A lot of Ralph Lauren breezes through here, and the crowd varies widely. The food is seasonal and very good. Standouts include the braised lamb shank, pan-seared halibut, the pear cobbler, generous salads, and tangy sorbets. $$$

James Lane Cafe
74 James Lane
631-324-7100
Here's an attractive restaurant in a country setting just as you turn into downtown East Hampton. It used to be called the Hedges Inn. If your credit line allows, you can stay over after dining. The menu is highlighted by broiled crab cakes, lobsters, the grilled veal chop with preserved lemon marinade and wild mushroom risotto, pine nut-crusted sea scallops, and the grilled sirloin steak. Sauteed broccoli rabe and garlic-mashed potatoes suit the main courses. $$$

Laundry
31 Race Lane
631-324-3199
Laundry keeps spinning along. It has undergone several lives since 1980. The latest at this contemporary-looking eatery is very good. The cuisine: a mix of new American and European. Tasty crab cakes, cornmeal-dusted skate wing, sauteed striped bass with sweet corn, roasted chicken with garlicky mashed potatoes, and a delectable strawberry shortcake. Bring lots of quarters. $$$

The Maidstone Arms
207 Main St.
631-324-5006
The Maidstone Arms, the grande dame of Main Street, has undergone a facelift in recent years. It's a sunnier spot, cozy and attractive year-round. The food is lively, new American fare. Some favorites: duck with a mandarin-coffee glaze, grilled peppered tuna with caramelized fennel; seared foie gras with sultanas and Sauternes, rack of lamb with curry sauce. $$$

Nick & Toni's
136 N. Main St.
631-324-3550
The haute hangout of celebrities big and small, Nick & Toni's has some of the Hamptons' most-sought tables. The food can be very good and the staff has become much friendlier over the years. The wood-burning oven specials are recommended, especially the whole fish, loin of veal, steaks and free-range chicken. Pastas trail. Spielberg sightings. $$$

The Palm at
The Huntting Inn
94 Main St.
631-324-0411
A bucolic branch of the grand chain of steak houses, The Palm is among the top five or six steakeries on Long Island. And it places that high for huge lobsters , too. They're better than the ones at your favorite fish house. Begin with the shrimp or crab meat cocktail, try a sliced tomato and onion salad and go down the menu in this order: double strip steak

for two; solo strip; the jumbo broiled lobster; sliced steak à la stone; filet mignon; chopped steak; prime rib; lamb chops. On the side: cottage fries, hash-browns, creamed spinach. The cheesecake is good. $$$

Peconic Coast
103 Montauk Highway
631-324-6772

A friendly and very good new American restaurant, with a style that's both warm and cool. Exposed brick, handsome wood bar, fine service, better food. Winners include red Peconic clam chowder; the tower of lobster, avocado, mushroom and tomato; sauteed halibut with carrot-ginger sauce; pan-roasted snapper; sauteed calf's liver with black grapes and vermouth, and a savory meat loaf. $$$

Riccardo's Seafood House
313 Three Mile Harbor Rd.
631-324-0000

South American fare with a Chilean twist . The bright, fresh restaurant has a serene water view, too. Colorful dishes include the clam-and-monkfish chowder, ceviche of scallops and shrimp, striped bass poached with tomatoes and vegetables, and a snappy fish and chips made with bass. Bring on the pisco sours. $$$

Rowdy Hall
40 Main St.
631-324-8555

This Anglo-Gallic hybrid brings together pub and bistro with equal ease. You could easily become a regular. Try the onion soup, sealed under a lid of Gruyère. Salads are winners, especially the Roquefort-walnut number with endive and Boston lettuce. Fish and chips is made with cod; the fries have Guinness in the batter. The croque monsieur is addictive. Or try the fried oyster sandwich. And there's the obligatory Rowdyburger. $$

Santa Fe Junction
8 Fresno Place
631-324-8700

Some southwestern sparks reach the East End via this joint. The fun starts with the mesquite-grilled skirt steak fajitas and grilled tortilla pizza as well as the char-grilled pork chops with chili chutney. $$

Saracen
108 Montauk Highway, in Wainscott, just west of East Hampton
631-537-6255

The sunny and stylish successor to Sapore di Mare, which generated the wave of extra-virgin olive oil that overtook Hamptons' dining, presents expertly prepared seafood, snappy pastas and a finely tuned buzz. The decor is molto

Hampton: a tribute to white, with light wood accents and ample terra cotta. You'll delight in the grilled ripe figs stuffed with prosciutto and Gorgonzola and the fried zucchini flowers packed with warm mozzarella. Next, fusilli tossed with cubes of swordfish in red sauce, or the grilled veal chop with roasted peppers and onions, or any of the grilled finfish. Fruit tarts and sorbets are the right finales. $$$

Tsunami
44 Three Mile Harbor Rd.
631-329-6000
Pan-Asian cooking sparks this part-restaurant, part-club scene. The decor is suitably exotic, with a rush of gold and orange and rose that leads to a copper bar. Good choices are the Indonesian, pepper-crusted shell steak; pesto-rubbed tuna with roasted peppers, mango and toasted sesame, and chicken satay. $$$

Turtle Crossing
221 Pantigo Rd. (Route 27)
631-324-7166
First-class, hardwood-smoked barbecue will ensure return visits, whether to eat in or take out. Spend a profitable session downing sliced brisket, pulled pork, chicken, duck, combinations thereof, at very civilized prices. Snappy chili, and enough "fancy wraps" to keep you going strong. $

Greenport

Aldo's
103-105 Front St.
631-477-1699
The veteran Mediterranean eatery has taken a Japanese turn. Now, you have sushi at Aldo's. The menu is a familiar tour of the raw and the cooked. The inside-out and special rolls are recommended. The "North Fork roll" means smoked salmon, asparagus and cream cheese; the "Hampton roll," tuna, asparagus and caviar. But try the spicy tuna, eel and cucumber, and chopped scallop rolls instead. Across the street is Aldo's biscotti emporium. The pistachio, hazelnut, almond and dark chocolate-dipped biscotti are tasty souvenirs, if they ever make it home. $$

Antares Cafe
2530 Manhanset Ave.,
in the Brewer Yacht Yard
631-477-8839
An ambitious establishment, with a modest water view and a kitchen vibrant as the bold, stellar red that colors the dining room. A menu from the peerless Paris restaurant Taillevent is among the decorations; if you have a role model, make it the best. Friendly and attentive staff members add to the mood of the place. Tomato-and-sorrel soup, butternut squash soup, and soy-glazed whiting with lentil wafers and

Antares Cafe: a star in Greenport.

grapefruit are typical appetizers. Roasted saddle of lamb, confit of Long Island duck, and roasted lobster with a sauce based on Bedell Cellars' ice wine head the main courses. Conclude with a Champagne-and-raspberry sorbet. $$$

Bistro Blue
1410 Manhanset Ave., at the
Stirling Harbor Marina
631-477-3940
Pretty and popular, this is a pleasing eatery for wraps and burgers as well as local seafood and uncomplicated pastas. Some recommendations: crab cakes; macadamia nut-crusted snapper with oranges; seared or grilled yellowfin tuna; the pork paillard with garlicky mashed potatoes; and the individual pizzas, which include a Tuscan pie sporting prosciutto, pine nuts and Fontina cheese. Lots of martinis, in many guises, are served here. $$

Bruce's
208 Main St.
631-477-0023
A spirited little cafe for casual dishes, and a respectable source for cheeses and take-out fare. The omelets and sandwiches, soups and salads, muffins and scones will keep you busy while reading the newspaper. $

Chowder Pot Pub
104 Third St.
631- 477-1345
A friendly joint. Popular for the prime rib special, burgers in bulk, and Samuel Adams brews. Don't complicate things. $

Claudio's
111 Main St.
631-477-0627
Claudio's has a terrific location, and is the cornerstone of a local dining empire in Greenport. Be sure to order carefully; the plainer the better. $$$

Coronet
Main and Front Streets
631-477-9834
The corner luncheonette, and a reminder of the way things used to be. The eatery does have a time-capsule quality. And it's a genial, often-busy place to spend your lunch money on Yankee bean soup, assorted chowders and lobster salad. $

Desiderio's
400 Main St.
631- 477-2828
Satisyfing pizzas and hero sandwiches, and a familiar assortment of straightforward red-sauce dishes. $

The Greenport Tea Company
119A Main St.
631-477-8744
Finger sandwiches, quiche, Irish smoked salmon, clam pie, and "high tea" scones are the light attractions at this smile of an eatery. You won't mistake the establishment for a branch of Mariage Frères, but on the North Fork it's a welcome venture and not too cutesy. $

Hans' Wursthaus
45 Front St.
631- 477-8744
The casual cousin of Hans' Gasthaus is notable for the wurstburger, which is a grilled bratwurst patty with sauteed onions. The smoked pork and the "landsmann omelette" with potato pancakes will give you stamina for the rest of the day. $

Hellenic Snack Bar
Main Road, East Marion
631-477-0138
A welcoming Greek eatery. Recommended: broiled porgy, fried whiting, moussaka, skordalia, taramosalata, stuffed grape leaves and baklava. $

Ile de Beauté
314 Main St.
631-477-2822
A charming restaurant and crêperie, with good food and service. The variety of crêpes ranges from the sweet to the savory, and totals 110. The Roquefort production is especially tasty. A bowl of onion soup suits the place, too. Dine late, have a Champagne brunch, a casual lunch. It's dependable for all. $$

Rhumb Line
34-36 Front St.
631-477-9883
For a joint with a nautical theme, it's surprising that the better fare is a grilled strip steak or broiled lamb chops. Elsewhere, there are warning signs of the ersatz and the overdone: chicken cordon bleu, deep-fried mozzarella sticks, fried shrimp, baked clams. If you must, consider the catch of the day. $$

Jamesport

Cliff's Elbow Room
Main Road (Route 25)
631-722-3292
You go to any of the Cliff's establishments for one thing: the marinated steak. It's big, slightly sweet, deftly charred. If you like it, you love it. After that, the stuff is pretty routine. $$

Jamesport Country Kitchen
Main Road (Route 25)
631-722-3537
The kitchen has a cozy niche in wine country. It has all the requisite charm, and the two small dining rooms feel like part of an old home. Crab cakes and salmon cakes, duck with cranberry-pear relish, and chicken salad are good. At dinnertime, the roast duckling and grilled tuna are highlights. Forgo pastas, burgers, and the overly ambitious. $$

Laurel

Cliff's Elbow Too
Franklinville Road, off
Route 25
631-298-3262
The steak, revisited. $$

Mattituck

The Heritage Inn
14560 Main Rd. (Route 25)
631-298-4800
A country house with New Englandy good looks and good, American-continental fare. Among the commendable dishes are the corn-and-lobster chowder, grilled veal chop, rack of lamb, steamed or broiled lobster, and bread pudding with bourbon and caramel sauce. $$$

The Magic Fountain
3835 Main Rd. (Route 25)
631-298-5225
Stop here and you'll conclude that the best eating in Mattituck is ice cream, and this is the place to have it. In season, typically 30 flavors are available; off-season, 20. Pick one at random, and take some home, too. Mint chip, pumpkin, coconut, peach, strawberry and vanilla are some of the stars. $

Old Mill Inn
West Mill Road, off Cox Neck
Road and Route 48
631-298-8080
It's a waterfront site, and that's the inn's primary attrac-

tion. The American-continental food is satisfactory. The steaks and the pastas are popular items. So's the tap room. Feel free to get here by boat. $$

Riverhead

Lobster Roll/Northside
3225 Sound Ave.
631-369-3039
The Lobster Roll has long been a mainstay along the Napeague stretch en route to Montauk. Here's the North Fork branch. The namesake roll is good lobster salad on a hot dog bun. The fried seafood can be crisp or limp, depending on your luck. Fruit pies are the obligatory desserts. $

Polonez
123 Main St.
631-369-8878
When the light and the nouveau have gotten to you, come to Polonez for the cure. Soulful, rustic food to strengthen you for a 12-month winter. Eggs and kielbasa for breakfast, Ukrainian borscht and potato-and-cheese pierogis for lunch, beef with horseradish sauce and potato pancakes for dinner. Fill out the day with take-out blintzes, stuffed cabbage and pork stew. $$

Riverhead Grill
85 E. Main St.
631-727-8495
The '50s endure on the Grill's menu and in its style. The fare

is homey and generally good. Stay with the meat loaf, a fresh ham sandwich, pot roast, corned beef; skip baked flounder, fried scallops, goulash and noodles and the Reuben sandwich. Breakfast is a dependable meal. $

Snowflake
1148 W. Main St.
631-727-4394
Great ice cream, with creative and superb flavors-of-the-week, and classic soft-serve. If ever there was a case for stashing a cooler in the trunk before leaving home, this is it. Peerless peach, luscious cannoli, a nostalgic riff on Creamsicle, chocolatey Peconic Swamp Thing, and vanilla are a few favorites that might keep you from experimenting with anything new. $

Spicy's
225 W. Main St.
631-727-2781
Sort of post-genteel, Spicy's definitely won't grab you with its rundown appearance. But the barbecue is zesty and very good, whether you're eating in or taking out. Chopped beef and pork, ribs, chicken. $

Sag Harbor

The American Hotel
Main Street
631-725-3535
The American Hotel presides formally over dining out in Sag

Harbor. The establishment dates to 1846. It undergoes periodic mood changes, and the management style veers from testy to temperate. The food, however, can be very good. Grilled lamb chops, sauteed foie gras, a shellfish platter. The wine list is the size of an 18th Century novel and provides ample reading material, right to left. $$$

B. Smith's
Long Wharf Marina, at the end of Main Street
631-725-5858
The marina setting offers a wonderful view at sunset, or on any summer day. This is TV personality and doyenne d'entertaining Barbara Smith's East End production. Among the tasty dishes: roast tomato gazpacho, lobster salad, pork chops with hamhock gravy and fried plantains. $$$

The Beacon
8 W. Water St.
631-725-7088
A lovely water view and stirring Euro, Asian and American cooking illuminate The Beacon, among the more Hamptonesque additions downtown. Sichuan-style confit of duck, moist and slightly spicy, is paired with somen noodle salad. A salad of endive, lettuces, quince and blue cheese refreshes. Roasted monkfish with Savoy cabbage, fennel, tomatoes and sweet corn bouillon heads the main courses,

rivaled by a buttery steamed lobster. Showcase desserts, starting with a lemony crêpe-soufflé. $$$

Estia's Little Kitchen
Bridgehampton-Sag Harbor Tpke.
631-725-1045
The westerly offshoot of Estia in Amagansett, this casual spot sports wraps, omelets and good fish cakes. Breakfast is the best meal, with blueberry pancakes. Fish cakes and potato-crusted flounder spur dinner. $

Paradise Cafe
126 Main St. in BookHampton
631-725-6080
Walk through the newest edition of BookHampton and you'll find this best-seller. Paradise Cafe is the cooking section come alive, to a vaguely Art Deco theme. Nori-wrapped salmon with a wasabi-red onion puree; grilled, prosciutto-clad scallops; the pan-roasted guinea hen accented with rosemary; and snappy, five-spice duck are first-rate main courses. Lavender-scented creme brulee leads the sweets. $$$

Sagaponack
Alison by the Beach
3593 Montauk Hwy.
631-537-7100
This is Alison on Dominick ... on vacation. The summertime scion of the downtown

The Plaza Cafe: the Hamptons' catch of the day.

Manhattan restaurant, complete with its stylized Cocteau "A" signature. Out here, the initial on the business card sports a beach umbrella. You'll like the roasted chicken with morels, the roasted beet salad, house-cured salmon with fennel and watercress, monkfish with gingered vegetables, and the artful desserts. $$$

Old Stove Pub
3516 Montauk Hwy.
631-537-3300
The Old Stove Pub proclaims reality among the Hampton food fantasies. Resolutely anti-chic, the restaurant hints at what used to be around, real or imagined, before citification set in. Celebrities arrive in season. Begin with the Greek appetizers: bubbling saganaki, saline and creamy taramosalata. Respectable moussaka and

pastitsio are the bargain entrees. The charred beef has a wonderful, old-fashioned flavor. Veal chops and lamb chops are grand, too. No garnishes. Just meat. Everything else is on the side, which is to say à la carte. $$$

Sayville
Collins & Main
100 Old South Main St.
631-563-0805
The area's intersection of good food and good times. The over-size photos of vintage Sayville and the joint's easygoing style have considerable appeal. The food, however, has more ups and downs than Dow Jones. Highlights include the filet mignon with Bordelaise sauce, roasted chicken on Savoy cabbage, and double-cut pork chop with red cabbage. $$

The Sayville Inn
199 Middle Rd.
631-567-0033
Well, it's old all right, dating to the 1880s. Casual and to the point, the Inn is best for burgers and fries, onion soup, turkey pot pie. Resist the extremes, whether mozzarella sticks or roast duck with peppercorn sauce. $$

Southampton

Barrister's
36 Main St.
631-6206
Informal and friendly, Barrister's is all right for hamburgers, wraps, salads, simpler pastas or a steak. The bar gets pretty noisy. Best for lunch. $$

basilico
10 Windmill Lane
631-283-7987
Lower-case basilico grows higher and higher. It's the essence of summertime in the Hamptons, and the reigning Tuscan-style restaurant. Celebrities make cameo appearances. All may savor the vitello tonnato, rigatoni with sweet sausage and pink sauce, and fettuccine Bolognese. Sometimes, a Cajun dish will pop up, or a more exotic marriage of seafood and fruit will enter the competition. But the tiramisu reminds you why the dessert caught on. And the finale of sweet wine and biscot-

ti is as stellar as it was in the summer of 1990. $$$

The Plaza Cafe
61 Hill St.
631-283-9323
Fin for fin, the best seafood restaurant in the Hamptons. The dining room is serene and the kitchen is exciting. Shepherd's pie made with lobster, shrimp and shiitake mushrooms; horseradish-crusted cod with garlic-mashed potatoes; tuna tartare; and sesame-crusted tuna with cellophane noodles and baby bok choy point the direction. For the landlocked, they prepare an excellent herb-crusted rack of lamb with a morel sauce. $$$

red/bar brasserie
210 Hampton Rd.
631-283-0704
White-hot when it opened, red/bar, another lower-case star, has been a tough reservation since day one. It's noisy, lively and very NYC. A Manhattan branch opened last year. The flavorful entrees include baked halibut, pan-roasted chicken, and pine nut-crusted rack of lamb. The fig-and-raspberry tart and the lemon-poppy-seed cake also are very good. $$$

75 Main
75 Main St.
631-283-7575
Chefs change, 75 Main stays

the same. A very good, informal restaurant. You can have a satisfying hamburger or dive into tournedos Rossini and steak au poivre. Other attractions: cedar-planked salmon, grilled pork tenderloin, garlic-crusted chicken. The pizzas improve on the pastas. Recommended for both brunch and dinner. $$

Sant Ambroeus
30 Main St.
631-283-1233

The country outpost of New York and Milan's casa gelati. A four-scoop showcase that's also a very good restaurant. Spaghetti alla carbonara and veal chop Milanese are among the dependable main courses. Move on to dessert and anything chocolate. As for the gelati: nutty crocantino, invigorating passion fruit, tangy grapefruit and lemon, luscious hazelnut. Worth visiting just to see the stunning cakes, too. Only the blindfolded could cut them without guilt. The restaurant is $$$; gelati to go, $.

Southampton Publick House
40 Bowden Square
631-283-2800

The local microbrewery and restaurant does well in both categories, at a venerable address where once the dry martini and the double Scotch reigned for celebrities of all stripes. Enjoy the hamburger and the ribs. The house sampler of brews is an ideal introduction. There's heady porter, yeasty "Southampton Gold," and tasty, unfiltered wheat beer. The offerings change often. $$

Southold
Coeur des Vignes
57225 Main Rd. (Route 25)
631-765-2656

This French restaurant should be a lot better. The presentations are attractive, the service competent, and the Victorian style apropos. But order carefully, the food is inconsistent. Try filet mignon with Bearnaise sauce rather than the rack of lamb; spiced duck breast with pistachios instead of Dover sole meunière. And forgo the frogs' legs and escargots. $$$

Pagano's
Main Road (Route 25)
631-765-6109

Informal, and better for the pizzas and the calzones than the pastas and the seafood. Try the white pizza, with ricotta, mozzarella and Romano cheese; or one of the deep-dish tributes to Chicago-style pizza. $

The Rotisserie and Smokehouse of Southold
Route 48, east of Youngs Avenue
631-765-9655

John C. Ross, for many years the most celebrated chef on the North Fork, closed his main

The Rotisserie: chef John C. Ross goes casual.

restaurant but continues to run this modest, full-flavored eatery. It's more take-out than eat-in. But there are a few tables at which you may revel in his hickory-roasted duck legs, rotisserie chicken, fried chicken, pork barbecue and baby back ribs. For the vegetarian: rotisserie potatoes, mashed potatoes, creamed spinach, cornbread stuffing and baked beans. $

**The Seafood Barge
62980 Main Rd., opposite
Port of Egypt marina
631-765-1010**
The barge carries its weight in lobsters. Finfish, too. The latest

incarnation of the place is very good, with a splashy selection of sushi. The swordfish au poivre and the steamed lobster are winners. Among the satisfying openers are pastrami-smoked salmon and crab cakes with a cilantro-mint vinaigrette. Skip the fried stuff, pastas, "bouillabaisse." $$

Water Mill

**Mirko's
Water Mill Square
631-726-4444**
Mirko's improves each year with evocative, enticing food, in a comfortable, warm setting. Service is superior. And so are

dishes such as the Croatian sweet-sour stuffed cabbage, smoked salmon trout with wasabi-shot crème fraîche, Moroccan-spiced grilled salmon and roast duck breast with a sauce that hints of honey and lime. The desserts are uniformly excellent. But you'll be partial to the sorbets. $$$

Robert's
755 Montauk Hwy.
631-726-7171
Robert's was the big hit of summer '99. The place has tossed a few curves since then. But when the "Italian coastal" cookery is swimming along, the restaurant is a delight. The pastas include a fabulous fettuccine with fresh artichokes, asparagus and peas in cream sauce. Whole roasted sea bass with olives and Vernaccia wine, roast monkfish with artichokes and basil, and braised halibut sparked with mint vie for catch of the day. A tangy blood-orange sorbet is the right finale. $$$

Station Road
50 Station Rd.
631-726-3016
The successor to The Station Bistro adroitly pursues new American cooking. The site remains a beauty: a circa 1930 Long Island Railroad station transformed into a good-looking restaurant. Have your "Brief Encounter" with crab cakes crusted with sesame seeds and spiked with lemongrass; a lobster-and-yucca samosa; grilled blackfish with tropical fruit; and the rack of Australian lamb lightly seasoned with cumin and honey. They're all fine, as is a local berry shortcake. In a nod to the past, there's a terrific crème brûlée, too. $$$

Chapter 12

Stick Around

Sightseeing, lodging, shopping

Wineries and vineyards are pretty recent additions to the East End. The twin forks are dotted with history. The North Fork, bordered by Long Island Sound and Peconic Bay, and the South Fork, with some of the nation's finest beaches, make the region a classic summer destination, the sunniest in New York State.

A fall day trip to the North Fork or to the Hamptons is a familiar experience for many in the New York metropolitan area. So are an overnight stay, a weekend in the country and longer hot-weather visits.

What follows is a brief guide to lodging for those not fortunate enough to be invited to a friend's beachfront mansion or country estate. The listings of the bed-and-breakfasts, motels and local shops are directories, not reviews. The price range for lodging generally is from the lowest off-season cost per room to the highest peak-season cost, or minimum winter rates to maximum summer rates. The prices are subject to change.

In addition, this chapter covers notable sites unrelated to grapes in the communities where the wineries and vineyards are located. And a trip to the East End has to include a visit to at least one of the farm stands that sprout in season along Main Road, or Route 25, and Route 48, also known as North Road, on the North Fork, and on Montauk Highway, or Route 27, on the South Fork. You never know when you'll need a pint of berries or a juicy peach for the road.

What to See

Bridgehampton

Elaine Benson Gallery
Montauk Hwy. (Route 27)
631-537-3233
Contemporary art.

Bridgehampton
Historical Society
2368 Montauk Hwy.
(Route 27)
631-537-1088

Bridgehampton
Presbyterian Church
2429 Montauk Hwy.
(Route 27)
631-537-0863
Established in 1670.
Greek Revival building.

Cutchogue

Cutchogue Green
Historic Buildings
Main Road (Route 25)
631-734-7122
The buildings include the 1740 Wickham house, one of the old-est farmhouses on the North Fork and host to a quilt collection, and the Old House, which dates to 1649, making it among the oldest English-style houses in the state.

Cutchogue
Presbyterian Church
Main Street (Route 25)
Organized in 1732; built in 1853.

East Hampton

Clinton Academy and
Town House
151 Main St.
The East Hampton Historical Society oversees these 18th Century buildings. Clinton Academy, which opened in 1785, was among the first chartered secondary schools in the state. It prepared students for college or, for example, careers in sea-faring and surveying. The brick-and-wood building is Late Georgian style. The Town House

is Long Island's sole remaining town government meeting house from the Colonial period. The Town House also was a one-room schoolhouse for the three R's. The school was discontinued in 1845. Call the Historical Society at 631-324-6850

Green River Cemetery
Accabonac Road, Springs
Among the permanent residents are painters Jackson Pollock, Lee Krasner and Elaine de Kooning, and journalist A.J. Liebling.

Guild Hall
158 Main St.
631-324-0806
The fine arts museum offers its own collection, exhibits from artists, art classes, concerts and stage performances, readings, lectures and films. It opened in 1932. There are three galleries and gardens.

Home Sweet Home Museum
14 James Lane
631-324-0713
The saltbox house and the windmill are landmarks. The former dates back to the 17th Century; the latter, the 18th. It was the residence of John Howard Payne, who wrote the title song. The place also has been immortalized by Department 56's Snow Village collection. Ceramics and furniture are inside.

Hook Mill
Montauk Highway
631-324-4150
A working mill, open to the public for tours. It dates to the early 19th Century.

Mulford Farm
10 James Lane
631-324-6850
This was a farm as early as 1680 and was the residence of the Mulford family through 10 generations. It's a museum of 18th Century home and farm life. The Mulford barn, built in 1721, is among the most intact buildings of the period in the state. The farm is listed in the National Register of Historic Places.

Old East Hampton Cemetery
Main Street
Lion Gardiner, the first settler of Gardiner's Island, rests here amid the impressive stonework, as do artists Thomas Moran and Mary Nimmo Moran. Tombstones date to the 17th Century.

Osborn-Jackson House
101 Main St.
631-324-6850
The East Hampton Historical Society offices are situated in this 18th Century colonial home.

The Pollock-Krasner House
and Study Center
830 Fireplace Rd., Springs
631-324-4929
This is the former studio and residence of artists Jackson

Pollock and Lee Krasner. The drips of paint are part of the history at the site, near Accabonac Harbor. Tours are by appointment only. The center presents exhibits and lectures.

Vered Gallery
68 Park Place Passage
631-324-3303
Devoted to paintings, photographs and sculpture.

Greenport

East End Seaport Museum
and Maritime Foundation
Third Street at the ferry dock
631-477-2100
Submarine, lighthouse, shipbuilding artifacts and models, as well as an aquarium of local fish.

Greenport Carousel
Front Street
A vintage merry-go-round, from the 1920s. Yes, you can try to grab the brass ring while spinning on the 40-foot carousel. Expected to be relocated closer to the harbor area by summer 2001. Hours not set yet.

Railroad Museum
of Long Island
Ferry dock
631-477-0439
The easterly branch of the museum, housed in the historic railroad depot. Among the displays is a 1925 Long Island Railroad wooden caboose.

Hampton Bays

The Big Duck
Sears Bellows County Park
Route 24
631-852-8292
The Sphinx of Poultry stoically presides over Route 24. The Big Duck weighs in at 16,000 pounds of mesh and cement. It's roadside architecture of a high-flying order, and in the National Register of Historic Places. The quacker, complete with closed beak and impassive eyes, was built in 1931 by a Depression-rattled farmer intent on selling his ducks and eggs. Now, you enter a gift shop.

Mattituck

Mattituck Historical Society
Main Road (Route 25)
631-298-5248
Museum, tours.

Old Burying Ground.
Main Road (Route 25)
Graves of settlers.

Peconic

Goldsmith's Inlet County Park,
off Mill Road
631-854-4949
Sixty-acre park. Hiking trails, bird watching.

Riverhead

Atlantis Marine World
Main Street
631-208-9200
Aquarium includes 120,000-gallon shark tank, live coral reef.

Hallockville Museum Farm and Folklore Center
6038 Sound Ave.
631-298-5292
An eight-acre farm with exhibits, blacksmith and haysmith demonstrations, local history.

Indian Island County Park
Long Island Expressway exit 73 to Route 105
Facility encompasses 287 acres. Camp site, hiking, playground, picnic area.

Railroad Museum of Long Island
Railroad Avenue
631-727-7920
Exhibits include railroad cars, steam engine, combine, historic trains collection. There is a branch of the museum in Greenport.

Splish Splash Water Park
Long Island Expressway exit 72 West
631-727-3600
Sprawling 40 acres and sporting 16 slides, Splish Splash is the tri-state area's largest water theme park. Wave pool, children's pools, interactive play. There are height require-ments for some of the slides, and "proper bathing attire" is required. Adults, $29.95; visitors under 48 inches in height or more than 62 years old, $17.95; children 3 or younger, free. No charge for the tubes.

Suffolk County Historical Society
West Main Street
631-727-2881
Museum and research library.

Sag Harbor

Bay Street Theatre
Long Wharf
631-725-0818
Plays, cabaret acts.
Open year-round.

Old Custom House
Main Street
631-725-0250
First Long Island post office.
Dates to 1789.

Sag Harbor Whaling and Historical Museum
Garden Street
631-725-0770
Collection of whaling tools, ship models, artifacts. Building dates to 1845.

Whalers First Presbyterian Church
44 Union St.
Established in 1766; present building designed in 1844.

Sagaponack

Madoo Garden
618 Main St.
631-537-8200
Gardens of artist-planter Robert
Dash. 18th Century building,
rose walk, Chinese bridge.

Southampton

First Presbyterian
Church of Southampton
Main Street
Established in 1640, it's the
oldest church in New York
State. Gothic Revival style.

Parrish Art Museum
Jobs Lane
631-283-2118
American art from the 19th and
20th centuries.

Pelletreau Silversmith Shop
78 Main St.
631-283-2494
Restored to the period of noted
Colonial silversmith and patriot
Elias Pelletreau, 1750-1810.

Southampton Cemetery
County Road 39
Established in 1885. Among
the interred is heavyweight
champion boxer Jack Dempsey.

Southampton
Historical Museum
17 Meeting House Lane
631-283-2494
In 19th Century whaler's home.
Antiques, artifacts, carriage
house, school house.

Southold

Custer Institute
Main Bayview Avenue
631-765-2626
Astronomy, star-gazing.

First Presbyterian
Church of Southold
Main Road (Route 25)
Founded in 1640 by Puritans
from Connecticut.

Horton Point Lighthouse
Lighthouse Road
Commissioned in 1790.

Old Burying Ground
Main Road (Route 25)
John Youngs, leader of the first
Puritan settlement, is interred
here.

Southold Historical Society
Museum
Main Road and Maple Lane
631-765-5500
Colonial building, Victorian
buildings, tours, consignment
shop.

Southold Indian Museum.
1080 Main Bayview Ave.
631-765-5577
Artifacts of Native American
life in the region. Lectures,
slide shows, exhibits.

Places to Stay

East End lodging covers a wide range of accommodations, from modest bed-and-breakfasts to full-scale waterfront resorts. Most of the bed-and-breakfasts offer a room with private bath and, of course, breakfasts of varying size. It's best to inquire in advance. Some require a minimum stay during the summer season. The resorts include beachfront houses, suites and rooms.

Aquebogue

Dreamers Cove Motel
Bay Avenue
631-722-3212
18 rooms, $65-$175.

J&S Reeve Summer Cottages
28 Whites Rd.
631-722-4096
7 cottages, 1-to-3 bedroom;
$99-$275.

Bridgehampton

Bridgehampton Inn
2266 Montauk Hwy.
631-537-3660
6 rooms, $175-$290, with
breakfast.

Enclave Inn
2668 Montauk Hwy.
631-537-0197
10 rooms, $75-$229, with weekend minimum stays.

Ludlow Greens
5 Ludlow Greens
631-537-5843
3 rooms, $120-$190, with
breakfast.

Morning Glory House
2623 Montauk Hwy.
631-537-2324
5 rooms, $200-$300.

Cutchogue

Country House B&B
Skunk Lane
631-734-5097
2 rooms in 1920s farmhouse,
$135-$150.

Cove View Inn B&B
5th Street & Peconic Bay,
New Suffolk
631-734-6392
4 rooms, $150-$250.

Freddy's House B&B
1535 New Suffolk Rd.
631-734-4180
2 rooms, $125-$165.

The Rhinelander B&B
26405 Main Rd.
631-734-4156
4 rooms, $125-$150.

Santorini Beach Hotel
3800 Duck Pond Rd.
631-734-6370
38 rooms, $129-$450,
with continental breakfast.

Top O' the Morning
26350 Main Rd.
631-734-5143
3 rooms, $125-$150,
with Irish breakfast.

East Hampton

The 1770 House
143 Main St.
631-324-1770
8 rooms, $165-$355.

Bassett House Inn
128 Montauk Hwy.
631-324-6127
12 rooms, $65-$195.

Dutch Motel
488 Montauk Hwy.
631-324-4550
22 rooms, 6 cottages, $65-$244.

East Hampton House
226 Pantigo Rd. (Route 27)
631-324-4300
52 rooms, $73-$300.

East Hampton Point
295 Three Mile Harbor Rd.
631-324-9191
13 townhouse units, studio to
2-bedroom, $100-$475.

The Hedges Inn
74 James Lane
631-324-7100
11 rooms, $175-$375; suite,
$475.

The Huntting Inn
94 Main St.
631-324-0410
19 rooms, $175-$375;
suite, $475.

Jeneen's Cottages
367 Three Mile Harbor Rd.
631-324-9024
12 efficiencies, $100-$275.

Lysander House
132 Main St.
631-329-9025
2 rooms, $200-$400.

The Maidstone Arms
207 Main St.
631- 324-5006
16 rooms, 3 cottages,
$148-$540.

Mill House Inn
31 N. Main St.
631-324-9766
8 rooms, $200-$450.

**Newtown House
Bed & Breakfast**
172 Newtown Lane
631-324-1858
4 rooms, $240-$300.

**The Pink House
Bed & Breakfast**
26 James Lane
631-324-3400
5 rooms, $135-$425.

Wainscott Village Inn
3720 Montauk Hwy.,
Wainscott
631-537-0878

24 rooms, $125-$400.

Greenport

Arbor View House B&B
8900 Main Rd. (Route 25),
East Marion
631-477-8696
3 rooms; $110-$185.

Bartlett House Inn
503 Front St.
631-477-0371
10 rooms, $105-$180,
with breakfast.

Drossos Motel
Main Road
631-477-1334
15 rooms, rates not available.

Edgewater
2072 Village Lane, Orient
631-323-3660
3 1-bedroom, waterfront
apartments; $850 per week in
season; $115 daily off-season.

Greenporter Motel
Front Street
631-477-0066
15 rooms, $215-$275;
Sunday rate, $95.

Morning Glory B&B
912 Main St.
631-477-3324
3 rooms, $135-$250,
with minimum stays.

Pleasant View Cottages
1305 Beach Rd.
631-477-4959

4 cottages, 2 with 1 bedroom, 2
with 2 bedrooms, $120-$185.

Quintessentials B&B Spa
8985 Main Rd. (Route 25),
East Marion
631-477-9400
5 rooms; $170-$190;
spa treatments.

Seahouse B&B
12910 Main Rd. (Route 25),
East Marion
631-477-0472
2 rooms; $100-$125.

Silver Sands Motel
Silvermere Road
631-477-1910
20 motel units, 20 beach houses,
$80-$250; $1,200 to $2,500
weekly. Waterfront.

Sound View Inn
Route 48
631-477-1910
49 rooms, $80-$250.

Townsend Manor Inn
714 Main St.
631-477-2000
23 rooms, $65-$200.

Treasure Island B&B
14909 Main Rd. (Route 25),
East Marion
631-477-2788
3 waterview suites; $295-$500.

Watson's by the Bay B&B
Bay Avenue
800-700-0426
3 rooms, $110 and up.

ɔɑ.   ᴄ

Moore's ᴗᴄ ᴀmer Cottages
Smith Lane
631-722-3814
7 cottages, minimum 1-week
stay in season, $750-$1,300.
Family-oriented.

Motel on the Bay
Front Street,
South Jamesport
18 rooms; waterview; $60-$220.

Vineyard Motor Inn
Main Road
631-722-4024
21 rooms, $55-$100.

Mattituck

Mattituck Motel
Bay Avenue
631-298-4131
19 rooms, $75-$125.

Peconic

The Belvedere B&B
3070 Peconic Lane
631-765-1799
3 rooms; $160-$200.

Home Port B&B
2500 Peconic Lane
631-765-1435
3 rooms in Victorian house,
$130-$150.

Riverhead

Budget Host Inn
30 East Moriches Rd.
near traffic circle
631-727-6200
68 rooms, $75-$139.

Greenview Inn
1433 W. Main St.
631-369-0093
50 rooms, $59-$99.

Ramada East End
1830 Main Rd. (Route 25)
631-369-2200
100 rooms, $159-$199.

Sag Harbor

The American Hotel
Main Street
631-725-3535
8 rooms, $145-$287,
with weekend minimum stays.

Baron's Cove Inn
West Water Street
631-725-2100
66 rooms, $95-$450.

Farrell's Country House
Marjorie Lane
631-725-0630
1 suite, $250.

Parker Guest House
Margaret Drive
631-725-7013
3 rooms, $185-$275,
with breakfast.

Sag Harbor Inn
West Water Street
631-725-2949
42 rooms, $85 to $350.

Southampton

1708 House
126 Main St.
631-287-1708.
12 rooms, $135-$475.

The Atlantic
1655 County Rd. 39
631-287-0908
62 rooms, $99-$450.

The Bentley
161 Hill Station Rd.
631-283-6100
38 suites, $99-$450.

The Capri
281 County Rd. 39A
631-283-4220
30 rooms, $99-$450.

Evergreen on Pine B&B
89 Pine St.
631-283-0564
5 rooms, $110-$325.

The Ivy B&B
244 N. Main St.
631-283-3233
5 rooms, $150-$395.

Mainstay B&B
579 Hill St.
631-283-4375
8 rooms, $145-$395.

Southampton Inn
91 Hill St.
631-283-6500
90 rooms, $119-$399.

Southampton Village Motel
315 Hampton Rd.
631-283-3034
10 rooms, $135-$250.

A Victorian Secret
104 Post Crossing
631-283-1623
2 rooms, $100-$150.

Village Latch Inn
101 Hill St.
631-283-2160
67 rooms, $125-$550.

Southold

Always Inn B&B
14580 Soundview Ave.
631-765-5344
2 rooms, $125-$150.

General Wayne Inn
1275 Cedar Beach Rd.
631-765-3344
23 rooms, $120-$180, breakfast
included. Dates to 1784.

Goose Creek Guesthouse
1475 Waterview Dr.
631-765-3356
3 rooms, $65-$90.

L'Hotel Coeur des Vignes
57225 Main Rd. (Route 25)
631-765-2656
4 rooms, $159-$195.

North Fork Motel
52325 Rte. 48
631-765-2080
30 rooms, $75-$135.

Shorecrest B&B
54300 North Rd.
631-765-1570
4 rooms, $125-$175.

Water Mill

Water Mill Guest House
Montauk Highway
631-726-4825
4 rooms, $100-$185,
with minimum stays.

Shopping and Souvenirs

Aquebogue
Island Treasures
523 Main Rd. (Route 25)
631-722-3100
Wind chimes, lighthouses, nautical items, gifts.

Bridgehampton
Penny Whistle Toys
Main Street (Route 27)
631-537-3875

The Rose House
Montauk Highway (Route 27)
631-537-2802
Antiques, home decoration.

Urban Archeology
Montauk Highway
631-537-0124
Artifacts, antiques, urban and otherwise, very big and small.

Cutchogue
Braun Seafood Co.
Main Road
631-734-7770
Oysters, etc.

Mary Casey Interiors
28320 Main Rd.
631-734-2532
Country dishware, home decorating.

The Down Home Store
Main Road
631-734-6565
Country items, prints, toys, jewelry, some antiques.

Wine Boutique
32645 Main Rd.
631-734-5221
Wine glasses, decanters, wine racks, winemaking equipment.

East Hampton
Architrove
74 Montauk Hwy.
631-329-2229
American, English and French antiques.

Banana Republic
8 Main St.
631-329-3142

Cashmere Hampton
85 Main St.
631-324-5000

Christmas East Hampton
70 Park Place Passage
631-324-5577

Coach Factory Store
69 Main St.
631-329-1777

DKNY
48 Newtown Lane
631-329-0555

English Country Antiques
21 Newtown Lane
631-329-5773
Furniture, chandeliers,
smaller items.

Dreesen's Excelsior Market
33 Newtown Lane
631-324-0465
For the old-fashioned doughnuts, among other edibles.

London Jewelers
2 Main St.
631-329-3939

Nuts About Chocolate
52 Main St.
631-329-5202

Obligato's Kids
55 Main St.
631-324-2233
Clothing.

Second Star
56 Newtown Lane
631-329-3750
Toys.

Victoria's Mother
43 Main St.
631-324-9507
Toys.

Greenport

Beall & Bell Antiques
18 South St.
631-477-8239
Mostly furniture.

Coastal Candleworks
110 Front St.
631-477-3515
Gifts, nautical products.

Curran's Irish Shop
119 Main St.
631-477-3503
China, glassware, pottery,
prints, clothing.

DiAngela
140 Main St.
631-477-1142
Gifts, leather, jewelry.

The Doofpot
308 Main St.
631-477-0344
Ceramics, glass, silk flowers,
jewelry.

Gifts by Lindon
218 Main St.
631-477-0165
Country gifts, prints, cards, toys.

Haag Todd Home
120 Front St.
631-477-0467
Nautical gifts, prints, arts
and crafts.

Old School House Antiques
68320 Main Rd. (Route 25)
631-477-8122

S.T. Preston
Main Street Wharf
631-477-1990
Nautical items, souvenirs.

Verbena
123 Main St.
631-477-4080
Home decorating,

Jamesport

Betty's Antiques
1176 Main Rd. (Route 25)
631-722-4473
Ephemera, paper.

Jamesport Country Store
Main Road (Route 25)
631-722-8048
Crafts, holiday items, foods,
furniture.

Mattituck

Bauer's Love Lane Shoppe
100 Love Lane
631-298-0204
Gift shop.

Cecily's Love Lane Gallery
Love Lane
631-298-8610
Prints, arts and crafts.

Love Lane Sweet Shop
163 Love Lane
631-298-2276

Riverhead

Briermere Farms
79 Sound Ave.
631-722-3931
Farm stand. But the real reason to come here is the fruit
pies, cookies, jams and jellies.
The crumb-capped pies and the
cream pies are local glories.
And the jams are a taste of
summer year-round.

Tanger Outlet Centers
Long Island Expressway
exit 73
800-482-6437
The 164 brand-name outlets
include Brooks Brothers,
Barneys New York, Eddie Bauer,
Cole Haan, Banana Republic,
Kenneth Cole, Donna Karan,
Dress Barn, Timberland, Bass,
Reebok, Carters, OshKosh
B'Gosh, Lenox, Mikasa, Corning
Revere, Oneida, Black & Decker,
Lechters; and Christmas shops;
gifts and crafts stores; dis-
count books; housewares.

Southampton

Christmas Southampton
20 Main St.
631-287-8787

Chrysalis Gallery
92 Main St.
631-287-1883
Local and international art.

Dansk Design
5 Main St.
631-287-2093

Hecho a Mano
46 Jobs Lane
631-283-7425
Hand-made gifts, home fur-
nishings.

Old Town Crossing
46 Main St.
631-283-7740
Imported antique furniture.

Story Time
20 Hampton Rd.
631-287-9035
Educational toys, books.

Villeroy & Boch
35 Main St.
631-283-7172
China, crystal.

Southold

Greenport Pottery
Main Road (Route 25)
631-477-1687
Wide range of well-crafted,
often colorful pottery, including
lamps, vases, bowls, tea and
coffee cups.

Peddlers Rest Antiques
45925 Main Rd. (Route 25)
631-765-3236
Furniture, silver, prints.

Wild Things Studios
53445 Main Rd. (Route 25)
631-765-9453
Gallery specializing in wildlife
art, floral designs, decorations.

Willow Hill Antiques
48405 Main Rd. (Route 25)
631-765-4124
Mostly furniture.

Windsong Country Store
Route 48
631-765-2817
Gifts, books, prints, candles,
wooden ducks, some antique
items.

Ye Olde Party Shoppe
53850 Main Rd. (Route 25)
631-765-5708
Toys, games, cards, stuffed
animals.

Farm Stands ... and a Dairy

Naturally, farm stands are at their fullest in summer and autumn. Many allow you to pick the fruit yourself. The short strawberry season in spring-early summer is a ripe time for picking. Peach and apple picking also are popular. In the fall, the cauliflower is the size of a bowling ball and unblemished. A 50-pound sack of potatoes is a heavy-weight souvenir.

Aquebogue

Little Chief
Main Road
(Route 25)
631-722-4369

McKay's
Main Road
(Route 25)
631-722-4142

Wells Homestead
Main Road
(Route 25)
631-722-3796

Cutchogue

Moonbeam Organic
5745 Alvah's Lane
631-734-5069

Satur Farms
3705 Alvah's Lane
631-734-2548

Wickham's Fruit Farm
Main Road
(Route 25)
631-734-6441

Jamesport

Harbes Family Farm
Main Road
(Route 25)
631-722-8546

Helen's
Main Road
(Route 25)
631-722-5847

Laurel

The Cider Mill
Main Road
(Route 25)
631-298-1140

Mattituck

Captain Kid Dairy
Route 48
631-298-5548

Harbes Family Farm
247 Sound Ave.
631-298-2054

Hooterville Farms
Main Road
(Route 25)

Tuthill
Route 48
631-298-8654

Peconic

Farmer Mike's
Main Road
(Route 25)
631-734-6956

Krupski's
Main Road
(Route 25)
631-734-6847

Punkinville USA
Route 48
631-734-5530

Sang Lee Farms
Route 48
631-734-7001

Wenofske's
Route 48
631-765-1617

Riverhead

Anderson Farms
Route 48
631-727-2559

Berezny's
Sound Avenue
631-722-3823

Briermere Farms
79 Sound Ave.
631-722-3391

Chick's
Farmstand
6045 Sound Ave.
631-298-5945

K.B. Farms
Sound Ave.
631-722-3823

Reeve Farm Stand
4138 Sound Ave.
631-727-1095

Rottkamp's
2287 Sound Ave.
631-727-1786

Young's Orchards
54 Sound Ave.
631-727-5363

Sagaponack

Schwenk's
Montauk Highway
(Route 27)

Wölffer
Farmstand
Montauk Highway
(Route 27)
631-537-9080.

Southold

Covey's Farm
Stand
Main Road
(Route 25)

Pete's Produce
Main Road
(Route 25)
631-477-8387

Water Mill

The Green Thumb
Montauk Highway
(Route 27)
631-726-1900

Hank Kraszewski
Farms
Route 39 and
Route 27
631-726-4964

The Milk Pail
Montauk Highway
(Route 27)
631-537-2565

Index

About the Author

Peter M. Gianotti is Newsday's restaurant critic and wine reviewer. He's the author of "Newsday's Guide to the Wines of Long Island" (1998); "Dining Out with Newsday" (1998, 1997); and co-author of "Newsday's Long Island Restaurant Guide" (1995, 1994) and "Eats NYC" (1995). Before reviewing restaurants, Gianotti was a Washington correspondent, economics writer, book critic and New York City reporter. Gianotti received his master's degree from Columbia University, where he also was a Bagehot Fellow, and his bachelor's degree from Fordham University, where he has taught journalism. He was born in Brooklyn, raised in Queens and lives on Long Island.

Editor: Kari Granville
Copy editor: Emily-Sue Sloane

Design Director: Bob Eisner
Art Director: Joseph Toscano

Photo Editor: Tony Jerome
Cover photo: Don Jacobsen
Back cover photo, pages 2-3, 15, 179,
and 183, J. Michael Dombroski
Pages 5, 8 and 21, David L. Pokress
Pages 11, 55, 79, 106, 117, 124-125, 132-133,
143 and 163, Tony Jerome
Page 153 (courtesy Post Liquors, Syosset), Bill Davis
Pages 160-161, Thomas Ferrara
Pages 171 and 176, Ken Spencer

Map: Linda McKenney

Prepress: Newsday Color Services
Production: Julian Stein

Notes

Notes

Notes

Notes